Kept out or opted out?

Understanding and combating financial exclusion

Elaine Kempson and Claire Whyley

The POLICY PRESS

First published in Great Britain in 1999 by

The Policy Press
34 Tyndall's Park Road
Bristol BS8 1PY
UK

Tel no   +44 (0)117 954 6800
Fax no +44 (0)117 973 7308
E-mail   tpp@bristol.ac.uk
http://www.bristol.ac.uk/Publications/TPP

© The Policy Press 1999

In association with the Joseph Rowntree Foundation

ISBN 1 86134 159 8

Elaine Kempson is Director and **Claire Whyley** is a Research Fellow at the Personal Finance Research Centre, University of Bristol.

The **Joseph Rowntree Foundation** has supported this project as part of its programme of research and innovative development projects, which it hopes will be of value to policy makers and practitioners. The facts presented and views expressed in this report are, however, those of the authors and not necessarily those of the Foundation.

Cover design by Qube Design Associates, Bristol.
Photograph used on front cover supplied by kind permission of www.johnbirdsall.co.uk
Printed in Great Britain by Hobbs the Printers Ltd, Southampton

Contents

Acknowledgements

This research could not have been completed without the help and support of a great many people and we would like to thank them for their hard work.

At the Personal Finance Research Centre (PFRC), University of Bristol, we would like to thank Sharon Collard for her invaluable contribution to the project and, in particular, the final report. Also, Professor Nigel Thrift and Dr Andrew Leyshon for reading and commenting on working papers. Our Advisory Group offered invaluable advice throughout the study. The group comprised:

Tony Baker, Deputy Director General
Association of British Insurers

Kelvin Baynton, Formerly, Head of Consumer Affairs, Personal Investment Authority

Adrian Coles, Director General
Building Societies Association

Amanda Jordan
Social Exclusion Unit

Susan Rice, Head of Branch Banking
Bank of Scotland

Tim Roberson, Consumer Economist
Office of Fair Trading

Theresa Williams, Principal Research Officer
Department of Social Security

We thank the Office of Fair Trading for allowing us access to their dataset on vulnerable consumers and Plus Four Research Ltd for undertaking the recruitment for the focus groups. We are also greatly indebted to the individuals who participated in the focus groups and who agreed to be interviewed in depth.

Finally, we are grateful to the Joseph Rowntree Foundation for providing financial support for the study and, in particular, to Derek Williams for his commitment and enthusiasm throughout the project.

Introduction

During the 1980s, retail financial markets expanded and more people gained access to a wider range of financial products than ever before. In the mid-1970s, less than half of all households had a current account – it is now about eight out of ten and many of these have facilities with their account that were not available 20 years ago (Kempson, 1994). Likewise, about a quarter of households in the early 1970s had credit facilities – a figure that had grown to seven out of ten in the space of two decades (Berthoud and Kempson, 1992). Moreover, forms of credit that were in their infancy in the early 1970s are now fairly commonplace. Two key factors influenced these developments: deregulation of the financial services sector, leading to greater competition, and developments in the use of information technology for risk assessment, which allow companies to accept a more diverse customer base than used to be the case.

Overall, these developments have benefited the majority of consumers, who now enjoy access to a wider range of financial products than in the past. But a minority of households lack even the most basic of financial product, such as a current account or home contents insurance. There is also mounting concern that these households are the most disadvantaged in society and that limited participation in financial services is contributing to the more general problem of social exclusion.

Despite this political and academic interest, we do not know how many people are affected, we are unaware of the problems they face in a society where there is widespread use of financial services, and we do not have an understanding of their unmet needs. This report is intended to fill these gaps in our knowledge.

Previous research

Previous research has found that large numbers of households lack basic financial products. Two out of ten households do not have a current bank or building society account (Kempson, 1994; Kempson and Whyley, 1998); a similar proportion do not have home contents insurance (Whyley et al, 1998). Around three out of ten have no savings at all (Kempson, 1998) and about the same number have not had access to consumer credit facilities in the previous year (Berthoud and Kempson, 1992). While we do not know the extent to which these are the same people, this earlier research does suggest a fair degree of overlap.

Existing research also demonstrates that financial exclusion is neither a single nor a straightforward process. Certainly it is not simply a matter of people being refused access outright. In fact, there seems to be a high degree of turnover. For example, about a third of the households lacking a current account had had one in the past, but had closed it down (Kempson and Whyley, 1998). Similarly, half of households who had no home contents insurance had been insured in the past but had let their policy lapse (Whyley et al, 1998). As a group, households who had given up a current account or home contents insurance differed quite markedly from those who had never had them.

A key question is whether the people who lack financial products are excluded from access or whether they self-exclude. Previous research suggests that, at the extremes, the answer is straightforward: a small minority are denied access to specific financial services by having facilities withdrawn or applications turned down. Equally a small minority do not want specific products under any circumstances (Kempson, 1994; Kempson and Whyley, 1998; Whyley et al, 1998).

Between these extremes, there is a grey area where people face barriers that encourage self-exclusion. Some people are deterred by price considerations, whether this be an unaffordable insurance premium, the high cost of credit sources available to people on low incomes or the risk of incurring charges by inadvertently overdrawing a current account. Others are deterred by the conditions attached to financial products, including people who are offered insurance policies with high excesses or containing exclusions that severely limit the policy's usefulness, and people who can only gain access to a current account with very limited facilities. Finally, there are people to whom none of the financial services are marketed and who have very little knowledge of financial products or how to go about getting them (Kempson, 1994; Kempson and Whyley, 1998; Whyley et al, 1998; Kempson, 1998).

Research aims and methods

The current research builds upon this earlier work to provide a detailed understanding of the extent and nature of financial exclusion, to identify unmet needs for financial products and how these needs can best be met. Within this, it has been designed to provide answers to the following more specific questions:

- How many households have restricted access to a wide range of financial products?

- What are the characteristics and circumstances of these households?

- In what ways are they excluded from financial services and how does this contribute to social exclusion more generally?

- What are their unmet needs for financial services?

- How might their needs be met and the trend towards financial exclusion be reversed?

The study involved three distinct but linked stages: secondary analysis of the *Family Resources Survey* to identify how many

households are affected and who they are; re-analysis of in-depth interviews with 87 households that had very limited use of financial products, to provide a detailed understanding of the processes of financial exclusion; and five focus groups to explore the extent and nature of unmet need for financial services. In addition, the Office of Fair Trading kindly gave us access to the statistical data they had collected through two modules of questions placed on the Office of National Statistics Omnibus Survey. Full details of the methods are given in Appendix B.

This report

Chapter 2 covers the extent of financial exclusion and the characteristics of both households who are completely outside financial services provision, as well as those on the margins of exclusion. It also examines the likelihood of households in different circumstances using financial products and identifies a hierarchy of access to individual financial products.

Following this, Chapter 3 looks in detail at the processes leading to financial exclusion, beginning with households who have disengaged and then turning to those who have never used any financial products.

Chapter 4 discusses the main unmet needs for financial services among those with low levels of use and the consequences of not having access to mainstream financial services. Chapter 5 focuses on ways of meeting these needs, separating out product design and the delivery of financial products.

Finally, Chapter 6 brings together the main findings of the research, draws out the implications for policy makers and practitioners, and identifies the scope for combating financial exclusion.

The term 'financial exclusion' is used in the report as it is widely accepted in the language of current debates on the broader processes of social exclusion, and we wanted to maintain the continuity of those debates. As a consequence, we use it as a generic term to describe all those who lack any financial products, regardless of the reason. In doing so, we are not suggesting that all these households experience direct exclusion because the financial services industry refuses to provide them with financial products. Rather, we recognise that they comprise a variety of characteristics, experiences and circumstances which cannot easily be summarised in the use of a single term. This includes people who are refused all products, those who decide freely not to use them, and those who self-exclude because of the inappropriateness of current products to households in their financial circumstances.

In addition to this report, three working papers have been produced which give, in greater detail, the results of the *Family Resources Survey* secondary analysis (Kempson and Whyley, 1999a); the depth interviews reanalysis (Kempson and Whyley, 1999b); and the focus groups (Whyley and Kempson, 1999).

The extent of financial exclusion

Around 1.5 million households in Britain (7%) have no mainstream financial products at all[1]. This means that they manage their household finances without a bank or building society account, have no money saved or invested, no private pension, no mortgage and are without any type of insurance. Moreover, a further one in five make only very limited use of financial services: one in 10 have just one financial product and a further one in 10 have two products. Most commonly, they have either a current account or a savings account with a bank or building society.

The situation does, however, vary across the country. Levels of non-use are highest in Scotland, where 13% of households have no financial products – twice the national average – and a further 25% have only one or two. Other localities with higher than average levels of non-use include the North and North West of England and Greater London. At the opposite end of the spectrum, the South East and East Anglia have far fewer households lacking access to financial services – in the South East, for example, only 3% of households have no financial products at all and a further 14% have just one or two.

Moreover, financial exclusion is concentrated among certain types of households in particular types of neighbourhood. And, at the same time, there are clear indications of the types of household most susceptible to being without financial products.

Who are the financially excluded?

The great majority (74%) of households without financial products are headed by a single person rather than a couple – including single people who live alone, both above and below pensionable age, and lone parents. Further, they are concentrated in social rented housing (84%) and, in England and Wales, almost half (47%) live in one of the 50 most deprived districts and boroughs according to the Department of the Environment, Transport and the Region's (DETR) index. It is, however, important to note that even areas with low overall rates of exclusion may have pockets of much higher levels concentrated within them (Table 2.1). Finally, households lacking financial products are poor. They are virtually all (94%) headed by someone who is not in paid work and, in two thirds of cases, the head of household has been without employment for six years or more. Consequently, seven in 10 are in receipt of Income Support and two thirds have net weekly incomes between £50 and £150 (Table 2.2).

Table 2.1: The characteristics of households with no financial products

column percentages

	No financial products	All households
Age of household head		
16-19	2	*
20-29	20	12
30-39	19	20
40-49	10	18
50-59	11	15
60-69	13	14
70-79	15	13
80+	10	7
Household type		
Single no children	22	14
Couple no children	5	17
Three + adults no children	1	7
Single pensioner	28	16
Couple pensioners	7	14
Lone parent	24	7
Couple with children	11	22
Three + adults with children	2	3
Ethnicity		
White	92	96
Black	4	2
Indian	*	1
Pakistani/Bangladeshi	2	*
Other	1	1
Age completed education (household head)		
16 or under	93	73
17-19	6	16
20 or over	1	11
Housing tenure		
Owned outright	3	26
Mortgagor	0	40
Local authority tenant	70	20
Housing association	14	5
Private tenant	13	9
Standard region		
North (including Cumbria)	8	6
Yorkshire and Humberside	8	9
North West	15	11
East Midlands	5	7
West Midlands	8	9
East Anglia	3	4
Greater London	15	11
South East (excluding London)	8	19
South West	5	9
Wales	7	6
Scotland	18	9
Local levels of deprivation**		
1 (Most deprived)	46	25
2	22	17
3	9	11
4	8	11
5	6	11
6	4	9
7 (Least deprived)	5	16
Weighted base	*1,751*	*26,435*

Source: *Family Resources Survey 1995/96*
*Less than 1%. ** Analysis based on the DETR Deprivation Index and restricted to England and Wales. Base: households with no financial products 1,324; all households 22,622.

Table 2.2: Socioeconomic circumstances of households with no financial products

column percentages

	No financial products	All households
Net weekly household income		
No income	*	1
£1–£50	1	1
£51–£100	26	11
£101–£150	41	17
£151–£200	20	14
£201–£300	11	20
£301–£400	1	14
£400–£500	*	9
more than £500	*	12
Net equivalent weekly household income		
No income	*	1
£1–£50	*	1
£51–£100	4	3
£101–£150	36	16
£151–£200	41	21
£201–£300	16	26
£301–£400	3	15
£400–£500	*	8
more than £500	*	9
Receipt of income–related benefit		
None	5	69
Council Tax Benefit only	2	5
Income Support only	1	2
Council Tax Benefit and Income Support	2	4
Housing Benefit only	3	2
Housing Benefit and Council Tax Benefit	17	5
Housing Benefit and Income Support	7	1
Housing Benefit, Council Tax Benefit and Income Support	63	12
Economic activity status (head of household)		
Self-employed	*	9
Full-time employment	4	42
Part-time employment	2	2
Unemployed	17	6
Retired	35	27
Sick/disabled	17	6
Student	1	1
Other inactive	24	7
Number of years since last worked (head of household)		
0	7	54
1	4	3
2	5	3
3	6	3
4	6	3
5	5	3
6–10	20	10
11–16	28	14
21 or more	19	7
Weighted base	*1,751*	*26,435*

Source: *Family Resources Survey 1995/96*

* Less than 1%.

What determines the likelihood of financial exclusion?

A review of the characteristics of households that are without financial products illustrates the nature of this population, and the types of households which are prominent in it. Another way of looking at this information, however, is to assess the *likelihood* of different types of households lacking financial products. This adds a further dimension to our understanding, by demonstrating which particular characteristics render people more or less likely to be outside the formal financial services system.

As Tables 2.3 and 2.4 show, certain groups have a high likelihood of having no, or very few, financial products. These include very young householders who are aged under 20 – many of whom will not *yet* have acquired many, if any, financial products – and at the other extreme, householders aged over 80, who would have moved into retirement by the time there was a rapid expansion of financial services.

In general, the younger a householder was when they left full-time education, the lower their likelihood of having financial products, although people who left school when they were 16 or younger did not, on the whole, have especially low levels of use. This, together with the findings in relation to income reported below, suggests that lack of education does not lead *directly* to low levels of use of financial products; it does so by increasing the likelihood of a low income.

Lone-parent households are highly likely to be very low users of financial products – with almost a quarter having none at all and another four out of 10 having just one or two products. The only other types of household with similarly low levels of usage are those headed by single pensioners. In other words, there is a greater likelihood of a female-headed household being excluded than one which is headed by a man.

There are also very clear ethnic differences. Usage of financial products is lowest in households classifying themselves as African-Caribbean or Black, Pakistani or Bangladeshi. Interestingly, however, Indian households are, if anything, even more likely to have financial products than white households.

We have already seen that the great majority of people without financial products live in the social rented sector, so it is not surprising to find that the likelihood of having financial products is especially low among both council and housing association tenants. In both cases around two out of 10 have no products at all, and half have very low levels of use.

As already noted, there are some very interesting geographical differences in the likelihood of households having financial products. In general, engagement with financial services markets is lowest in Scotland, followed by the North, Greater London and the North West, while it is highest in the South East. And, as might be expected, the likelihood of having financial products is linked to the overall level of deprivation within a local authority. Households living in the 50 local authorities in England and Wales with the highest levels of deprivation are more than six times as likely to have no financial products as those living in the 65 authorities with the least deprived populations.

Table 2.3: Number of financial products by household circumstances

row percentages

	Number of financial products**						Weighted base
	None	Low	Med low	Ave	Med high	High	
All households	*7*	*19*	*20*	*11*	*21*	*22*	*26,435*
Age of household head							
16-19	26	57	13	2	2	*	*112*
20-29	11	27	18	11	19	15	*3,211*
30-39	6	16	15	11	26	26	*5,272*
40-49	4	11	15	11	25	34	*4,738*
50-59	5	13	17	11	23	32	*3,982*
60-69	6	18	24	13	19	19	*3,813*
70-79	7	27	29	13	15	9	*3,522*
80+	10	39	27	8	10	6	*1,785*
Household type							
Single no children	11	25	20	11	19	14	*3,581*
Couple no children	2	10	15	12	28	33	*4,515*
Three+ adults no children	1	10	18	12	26	32	*1,911*
Single pensioner	12	37	28	9	9	5	*4,132*
Couple pensioners	3	16	27	15	21	18	*3,783*
Lone parent	23	42	17	7	7	4	*1,790*
Couple with children	3	11	14	10	27	35	*5,861*
Three+ adults with children	3	11	20	12	24	30	*862*
Ethnicity							
White	6	19	20	11	21	23	*25,215*
Black	16	37	22	8	10	7	*440*
Indian	3	17	26	16	18	19	*282*
Pakistani/Bangladeshi	14	42	29	7	6	2	*211*
Other	7	29	21	8	21	14	*287*
Age completed education (head of household)							
16 or under	8	23	22	11	19	16	*19,151*
17-19	2	11	15	11	26	35	*4,084*
20 or over	1	7	12	10	25	45	*2,939*
Housing tenure							
Owned outright	1	11	29	15	24	20	*6,818*
Mortgagor	*	1	12	14	33	40	*10,605*
Local authority tenant	23	51	19	4	2	1	*5,348*
Housing association	20	50	23	4	2	1	*1,190*
Private tenant	9	39	28	9	10	5	*2,474*
Standard region							
North (including Cumbria)	9	25	22	13	19	13	*1,619*
Yorkshire and Humberside	6	21	22	11	20	20	*2,305*
North West	9	21	20	11	20	19	*2,921*
East Midlands	5	19	19	12	22	23	*1,926*
West Midlands	6	20	20	11	21	22	*2,407*
East Anglia	4	17	19	12	25	23	*1,067*
Greater London	9	23	20	10	19	19	*2,961*
South East (excluding London)	3	14	17	11	24	32	*5,119*
South West	4	17	19	11	22	27	*2,297*
Wales	8	23	25	12	18	14	*1,455*
Scotland	13	25	19	10	19	15	*2,358*
Local levels of deprivation *							
1 (Most deprived)	11	27	20	11	16	15	*5,699*
2	7	22	23	11	21	16	*3,931*
3	5	19	21	13	24	19	*2,406*
4	4	15	20	13	23	25	*2,440*
5	4	13	18	11	23	31	*2,416*
6	2	13	16	11	24	34	*2,157*
7 (Least deprived)	2	12	17	11	24	34	*3,573*

Source: *Family Resources Survey 1995/96*

*Less than 1%. ** 'Low' =1 or 2 products; 'Medium-low' =3 or 4 products; 'Average' =5 products; 'Medium-high' =6 or 7 products; 'High' =8 or more products. ***Analysis based on the DETR Deprivation Index and restricted to England and Wales. Base: all households 22,622.

Table 2.4: Number of financial products by socioeconomic circumstances

row percentages

	Number of financial products**						Weighted base
	None	Low	Med low	Ave	Med high	High	
All households	*7*	*19*	*20*	*11*	*21*	*22*	*26,435*
Net weekly household income							
No income	2	18	17	13	22	27	*179*
£1–£50	6	26	28	13	18	9	*321*
£51–£100	16	39	29	6	8	3	*2,785*
£101–£150	15	37	26	10	9	4	*4,490*
£151–£200	9	29	25	13	17	8	*3,665*
£201–£300	4	15	22	16	26	18	*5,279*
£301–£400	*	6	16	12	34	32	*3,631*
£400–£500	*	3	8	10	31	48	*2,276*
more than £500	*	1	6	7	26	60	*3,193*
Net equivalent weekly household income							
No income	2	18	17	13	22	27	*179*
£1–£50	4	19	24	16	23	14	*213*
£51–£100	8	28	32	9	16	7	*791*
£101–£150	15	35	29	9	9	4	*4,058*
£151–£200	13	34	23	10	13	6	*5,282*
£201–£300	4	17	22	14	25	19	*6,769*
£301–£400	1	7	14	12	32	35	*3,976*
£400–£500	*	3	10	11	30	47	*2,127*
more than £500	*	2	6	8	25	59	*2,433*
Receipt of income-related benefit							
None	*	8	20	14	28	31	*18,289*
Council Tax Benefit only	2	24	39	13	15	6	*1,229*
Income Support only	4	18	27	13	21	18	*589*
Council Tax Benefit and Income Support	3	32	40	13	9	3	*974*
Housing Benefit only	13	62	21	2	2	*	*484*
Housing Benefit and Council Tax Benefit	21	58	17	3	1	*	*1,403*
Housing Benefit and Income Support	36	49	9	2	3	2	*365*
Housing Benefit, Council Tax Benefit and Income Support	35	55	9	*	*	*	*3,102*
Economic activity status (head of household)							
Self-employed	*	6	16	12	29	37	*2,386*
Full-time employment	*	9	16	12	29	34	*10,981*
Part-time employment	6	29	22	12	17	15	*442*
Unemployed	19	38	20	8	9	7	*1,565*
Retired	8	29	28	11	14	9	*7,262*
Sick/disabled	19	32	22	10	11	7	*1,573*
Student	8	40	28	8	10	6	*274*
Other inactive	22	32	14	6	12	14	*1,951*
Number of years since last worked (head of household)							
0	*	9	16	12	29	34	*13,809*
1	8	31	22	12	15	13	*832*
2	10	29	23	11	15	13	*810*
3	13	25	22	11	13	16	*739*
4	13	29	22	10	14	11	*782*
5	10	31	23	10	14	11	*714*
6-10	13	27	25	11	14	11	*2,455*
11-16	12	32	27	10	12	7	*3,620*
21 or more	16	39	25	8	9	4	*1,906*

Source: *Family Resources Survey 1995/96*

*Less than 1%. ** 'Low' =1 or 2 products; 'Medium-low' =3 or 4 products; 'Average' =5 products; 'Medium-high' =6 or 7 products.

The likelihood of having financial products is lowest in households with net incomes of between £50 and £150 a week – well over half of households with incomes at this level have, at most, two financial products. Moreover, the likelihood of a household having financial products falls steeply with income, so that only 2% of the highest income households have such low levels of use. There is a strong link between being out of work and having no or very few financial products, especially among households that are headed by someone who is unemployed, sick or disabled, or looking after the home or family on a full-time basis. Retired people and students are rather less affected.

What is more, the analysis suggests that people close down financial products during the first year or so that they are out of work. The proportion of people who have either no products at all, or only very low levels of use, barely increases with the length of time the household head has been out of work. This is consistent with findings from the second, qualitative stage of this research, detailed in Chapter 3.

Out of work tenants, claiming Housing Benefit and Income Support, have incredibly high levels of financial exclusion – more than a third have no products at all and half have very low levels of use. Low-income tenants not in receipt of Income Support, but getting other income-related benefits, fare only slightly better.

Predicting the likelihood of financial exclusion

So, we know that the likelihood of experiencing financial exclusion depends on household characteristics, housing and area effects, and socioeconomic circumstances. But many of the individual characteristics which affect the likelihood of a household being without financial products are interrelated. For example, a high proportion of council tenants are without paid employment; lone parents are especially likely to claim income-related benefits; and Pakistani and Bangladeshi households tend to have incomes that are well below average. From the analysis so far, we do not know the relative importance of each of the factors that influence the likelihood of a household being without financial products.

Nor do we know whether individual factors have a direct influence over the likelihood of a household being without, or whether they are simply a reflection of the indirect impact of other significant factors.

It is possible, however, to disentangle these effects by using the techniques of statistical modelling. Using logistic regression analysis we have determined the additional net effect of each significant individual characteristic, once we have held constant the influence of other related factors. In other words, by modelling, statistically, the effects of each of the significant variables on the likelihood of a household having no financial products, we could assess the extent to which these variables affect the 'odds' of financial exclusion (see Appendix A).

We ran two sets of models to predict the likelihood of financial exclusion. The first set predict the likelihood of a household being completely without financial products. We then replicated these models according to a broader definition of financial exclusion, which we describe as 'low levels of use', and which includes households with only one or two financial products *as well as* those who do not have any at all. While, broadly speaking, the same factors remain significant in explaining variations in a household's likelihood of financial exclusion according to both definitions, the extent and pattern of their influence changes in interesting ways.

Household economic circumstances

The key factors in predicting the likelihood of financial exclusion, on both definitions, related to household economic circumstances.

By far the most influential factor in predicting the likelihood of both non- and low-use of financial products was benefit status and, in particular, being an out-of-work tenant receiving Income Support, Housing Benefit and Council Tax Benefit (Appendix A, Table 1, Model 1A and Table 2, Model 2A). In comparison with a household not receiving any means-tested benefits, being in receipt of these three benefits increased the odds of having no financial products by 30 times, and of being a low user by a factor of 40. Even low-income tenants who were not on Income Support had a much greater likelihood of financial exclusion, according to either definition, relative to households who did not receive means-tested benefits.

Although the size of these effects was reduced when housing tenure was introduced into the models, its predictive power remained highly significant (Appendix A, Table 1, Model 1B and Table 2, Model 2B). In other words, receipt of means-tested benefits increases the odds of a household experiencing financial exclusion even when all its other characteristics and circumstances are taken into account.

Income level was also significant in increasing the odds of exclusion, although its effect was strongest in predicting the likelihood of being without financial products altogether. The chances of being a non-user of financial products increases steeply as income falls, so that households with net incomes below £150 a week were eight times as likely to fall into this category as those getting more than £300 a week (Appendix A, Table 1, Model 1A). Income was less influential in predicting the likelihood of a household being a low-user, but remained highly significant (Table 2, Model 2A).

Once again, the introduction of tenure into the model reduced the effect of income slightly, but it remained highly significant. The fact that both income and benefit status were so highly significant is especially striking. Clearly, receiving means-tested benefits reduces the likelihood of using financial products by even more than income level alone would predict.

The chances of being without any financial products increased with the length of time since the household head had last worked (Appendix A, Table 1). However, the odds of having fewer than two financial products was significantly *reduced* in households where the head had been without paid work for less than two years (Appendix A, Table 2). Taken together, this supports the hypothesis that when people move out of paid employment they retain financial products in the short term, although they may suspend use of them, but stop using them altogether the longer they are out of work. This process is, in fact, confirmed by qualitative analysis presented in Chapter 3.

Household characteristics

Some household characteristics are also significant in predicting the odds of financial exclusion, although their influence varies according to the definition used. Those predicting the likelihood of non-use of financial products include being a single non-pensioner household; having finished full-time education at age 16 or earlier; and being Pakistani or Bangladeshi (Appendix A, Table 2). Possible explanations are, in turn, that single-person households are newly formed and have yet to acquire any financial products; that people with low levels of education find financial products bewildering or off-putting; and that differences in language, religion or culture act as a barrier to Pakistani and Bangladeshi households using financial services.

The picture is very different, however, when we look at low-users, as well as non-users, of financial products (Appendix A, Table 2). Household composition (and in particular being a single non-pensioner) is barely significant in explaining low levels of use, nor is it particularly influential.

The age of the head of household has a much greater influence over the odds of a household making low use of financial products than it does on having none at all. Having very few products is clearly a particular issue for younger households. Those headed by someone aged under 20, for example, have almost 16 times the odds of having fewer than two financial products than a household headed by someone aged 40-49 (Appendix A, Table 2, Model 2A). Although this age effect reduces when tenure is added to the model, the under 20s remain more than eight times more likely to be low-users of financial products than older households (Appendix A, Table 2, Model 2B). These findings clearly support the hypothesis that many young people have simply not *yet* engaged with the financial services industry. However, despite the fact that very elderly householders – in their 70s and 80s – have a low likelihood of using financial services (Table 2.3), statistical modelling shows that being aged over 70 *decreases* the odds, especially of having no products at all (Appendix A, Table 1). In other words, it is most likely economic factors that explain the very low use of financial services among some very elderly people.

Ethnicity, too, has a far greater influence over the likelihood of a household having fewer than two financial products, than on having none at all. Pakistani and Bangladeshi households were the only minority ethnic group which had significantly higher odds of being completely without financial products (Appendix A, Table 1). Yet all minority ethnic groups, with the exception of Indians, had significantly higher odds of having fewer than two financial products (Table 2). Once again, it is Pakistani and Bangladeshi households that have the highest odds of being low-users – at least five times the odds of a comparable white household.

Area effects

There are some very interesting geographical effects, showing that levels of use of financial services depend not only on who you are but also where you live.

First, there are important regional differences in the likelihood of being completely without financial products, with Scottish households being three times as likely to be non-users as those in the South of England; Welsh households were twice as likely. In England, people living in the North and North West or in Greater London were almost twice as likely to have no financial products as those living in the South (Appendix A, Table 1, Model 1A). Although more regions are significant in the models of low levels of use, those with the greatest effects are, once again, Scotland, Wales and Greater London (Appendix A, Table 2, Model 2A).

Introducing tenure into the models does not, on the whole, greatly reduce these regional effects, while tenure itself is highly significant (Appendix A, Table 1, Model 1B and Table 2, Model 2B). Council tenants, for example, are seven times as likely to have no financial products and eight times as likely to be low-users as similar home-owning households.

In addition, living in one of the 50 most deprived local authorities in England doubles the chances of a household being without financial products and a similar influence on it being a low user of financial services. Predictably, adding the deprivation index reduces the regional effect indicating that it is partly due to the existence of pockets of deprivation (Appendix A, Table 1, Model 1C and Table 2, Model 2C).

It is important to note that the regional tenure, and deprivation index effects are not due to socioeconomic differences, as these are held constant in the models.

Access to financial products: a hierarchy

So far we have taken an overall view of whether people have any financial products at all, and how many products different types of household are likely to have. In this section we look at access to specific types of financial products, including current accounts, mortgages, a range of savings and investment products and a range of the most common types of insurance[2].

Although only one in 15 households have no financial products at all, rather more are without specific ones. Putting together information from the *Family Resources Survey* and the Office of Fair Trading survey of vulnerable consumers:

- between one in eight and one in five households do not have a current account;

- a quarter have no savings or investment products;

- about one in five have no insurance policies[3];

- a quarter have no credit commitments;

- and a third lack any pension provision.

If households have only one financial product, it is most likely to be either a current account (47%) or a savings account with a building society (21%) or bank (11%). When people have just two products, occupational pensions and structural insurance are added to the list. At the other end of the scale, the products most associated with high levels of use are PEPs, TESSAs, stocks and shares, unit trusts, mortgage payment protection policies, private medical insurance, personal accident policies, and insurance policies covering loss of earnings through sickness, redundancy or hospitalisation.

In general, access to individual financial products follows overall patterns of use. So, for example, low-income households have the lowest levels of current account holding, and this increases with rising household income. However, some individual products are much more sensitive than others to the factors that seem to increase overall levels of use of financial services. For example, households with net weekly incomes of more than £500 are 1.7 times as likely to have a current account as those with incomes between £51 and £100; but they are 29 times as likely to have an insurance policy to cover them for redundancy (although this particular product is likely to be far less relevant to people who have low incomes because they are not working). Similar effects were found with benefit status. Households claiming no income-related benefits were 2.6 times as likely to have a current account as those claiming Income Support, Housing Benefit *and* Council Tax Benefit; and they were 21 times as likely to be insured for redundancy.

The most 'sensitive' products included (in descending order of sensitivity):

- insurance for redundancy
- insurance for loss of earnings through sickness or disability
- private medical insurance, mortgage payment protection insurance
- PEPs
- Unit Trusts
- mortgages
- and TESSAs.

At the other end of the scale, the least 'sensitive' products were (in ascending order of sensitivity):

- current accounts
- building/structural insurance
- building society savings accounts
- Post Office accounts
- bank savings accounts
- National Savings accounts.

In other words, there is a hierarchy of access to financial products, beginning with current accounts at the bottom. People who are on the margins of financial services markets, if they have any money to spare, tend to keep it in the form of liquid savings. Beyond that, they either have an occupational pension or have insured the structure of their home – both products that they will have been strongly encouraged to take out. Insurance provision for ill-health or loss of income is very rare among those who are least likely to have financial products. This is especially worrying given the fact that they are the very people most likely to need cover.

Notes

[1] Based on the *Family Resources Survey*, which covers 23 different financial products. It does not, however, include either home contents insurance or consumer credit. These two types of product *were*, however, included in the Office of Fair Trading Omnibus data to which we were given access. Analysis of this data has confirmed the figures using the *Family Resources Survey*.

[2] Home contents insurance is omitted from the analysis as this data in the *Family Resources Survey* is incomplete.

[3] The *Family Resources Survey* shows that a third of households lack any of a wide range of types of policy, but does not ask all householders about home contents insurance. The Office of Fair Trading survey, however, found that 20% of all households had no contents insurance, a figure that is consistent with earlier research (Whyley et al, 1998).

3

The processes of financial exclusion

There is no single explanation for households having no, or very few, financial products. Although the great majority have never really used financial services to any degree, about a quarter of households with no financial products have had them in the past. This echoes earlier research which has shown that a third of individuals lacking a current account had used one previously but closed it down (Kempson and Whyley, 1998), while half of households with no home contents insurance policy had been insured at some time in the past but not renewed the policy (Whyley et al, 1998).

Equally, financial exclusion occurs for a variety of reasons and is neither a single nor a straightforward process. It encompasses outright exclusion in the form of companies refusing to accept certain households as their customers, and people who self-exclude by making an active and unconstrained choice not to have any financial products. For most, however, the process is much less clear-cut – it is the combined result of marketing, pricing and product design which leads certain groups not to use any financial services.

It is also a dynamic process and includes people for whom financial exclusion is a temporary state, and others for whom it seems likely to be long-lasting, if not lifelong.

Households that have never used financial services

About three quarters of households with no financial products have been without them for a considerable period of time[1]. They include:

- elderly people who have always lived on a low income;

- young householders who have not yet engaged with financial services;

- single (that is, never-married) women who became mothers at a very young age and are still caring for their children full-time;

- people who have always been on the margins of work;

- some ethnic minorities.

Several common traits are apparent among these five groups. First, there is a low level of awareness of financial products. Coupled with this is a mistrust of financial services, largely fuelled by adverse press stories about the mis-selling of financial products. Thirdly, because of who they are and where they live, no one has ever tried to sell them any financial products. As one woman put it, "You can't get anything, not even mail order, round here". Finally, these households tend to be marginalised in most other respects – they do not work and they live on run-down council estates where few of their neighbours are in work either.

Elderly, low-income households

Some elderly householders, in their 70s and 80s, have always operated in a cash economy and have managed all their lives without using financial services. They are about one in seven of all households with no financial products.

Case study 1: Elderly low–income households

A widow aged 78 had always dealt in cash, often keeping substantial amounts at home until it was needed. She had closed her building society account "because there is nothing to put in it". She did have a life insurance policy, taken out for her grandchildren, which had been sold to her by a door-to-door salesman; the premiums were also collected from her home. She had never used credit because she "... was brought up in the belief that if you wanted something you saved for it and then when you had enough money you went and bought what you wanted."

Typically, they have always had very low incomes and when younger had only one earner, generally in manual work, whose wages were paid in cash. Consequently, they have never needed a current account for wages and have operated a cash budget in order to keep control. Some may have been forced by employers to have an account for their wages and opted for a simple savings account; this was invariably closed down on retirement. Occasionally they have had life insurance policies, normally those sold door-to-door and generally taken out in the names of their children. However, they are often suspicious of financial services and have always been opposed to the use of credit. Finally, they have never had spare cash for savings, insurance or a private pension.

Young householders

Most young people acquire financial products gradually as their income rises, but many will have basic products such as a bank or building society account even before they set up their own household. Some young people, however, become householders without a secure income from employment and, consequently, have very little involvement with financial services. They represent about one in eight of households with no financial products. Two main factors limit their access.

First, they are considered a bad risk by many financial service providers, most commonly because they are in part-time or temporary employment. For example, one young woman who was working part-time to support herself while studying had problems getting access to current account facilities.

"I actually had difficulty in opening up a bank account. I tried Midlands and I also tried Barclays. And at the time I was working part-time and I had a problem opening an account. I think it was probably because I wasn't working full-time – and National Westminster was the only bank that would open an account for me."

This young woman, and others like her, will almost certainly start to make more use of financial services once she has found a secure job.

Second, some young people know very little about financial services and, as a consequence, do not seek to obtain products. They may have grown up in households that are on the margins of financial services, and their circumstances are such that they seem unlikely to use many, if any, financial products. This raises the importance of providing financial education in schools.

Single mothers

Unlike disengaged lone parents, who are more likely to be separated and divorced, lone mothers who have never engaged with financial services tend to be single and to have never co-habited with the father of their children. They are also very likely to have had their first child in their teens. Many are housed on hard-to-let council estates that are unattractive to financial service providers, come from families that use little in the way of financial products, and they themselves know very little about financial services. They account for about one in 10 of households with no financial products.

Case study 2: Single mothers

One single mother, who had worked on and off since the birth of her first child, had opened a savings account for her wages to be paid into, but had stopped using this when she gave up work to look after her youngest child. At 37, she had never applied for a current account because she thought she would not get one, and had never used credit in any form. She had almost no knowledge of potential sources of credit, including mail order, which is unusual for someone in her circumstances. She knew no one who had used anything other than the Social Fund to obtain credit.

These single mothers do not apply for financial services, such as a current account, consumer credit or insurance, in the belief that they will be refused them. Often this is based on received wisdom and, because few of their friends or neighbours have any financial products either, they believe the neighbourhood to be red-lined. Some have had applications for a particular product rejected, and this fuels the more generalised belief that "nothing like that is available to people like me".

Always on the margins of the labour market

The fourth group comprises slightly older households where the main wage-earner has been in and out of work. When they are in employment, it tends to be temporary, insecure or part-time.

Consequently, they are refused facilities such as bank accounts and credit when they apply for them, and on this basis do not even bother trying for others. Moreover, their circumstances are such that they can never afford to save or to take out insurance.

Households in these circumstances are the largest single group with no financial products. They comprise four out of 10 of the total. They include households of all types – single householders, lone parents, and couples with and without children. They also span a wide age range from 30 to 70.

Case study 3: Marginalised workers

A 38-year-old man lives with his wife, three of their children and a six-month grandchild. He had started out with a "damn good job" but was made redundant. Since then he has "had hundreds of jobs" and has virtually given up hope of ever getting a decent job again. He had recently declined a job with a security firm as the wages were only £2.15 an hour (equivalent to an annual salary of £4,400 for a 40 hour week).

During a brief spell as a self-employed taxi driver, he had opened a building society account, but he had never really used it. They had been refused hire purchase and had "never had any dealings with the banks. We've just never had enough money to, really". Likewise they had nothing in savings and no insurance of any kind. They did, however, borrow from two weekly moneylenders. When they

had a gas bill they could not pay they "were told to get in touch with [them] so we did, and the understanding was they only had unemployed people".

Ethnic minorities

Ethnic minorities – and certain Asian communities in particular – comprise the final group who have never really engaged with financial services, and represent a little under one in 20 of all households with no financial products. A number of interrelated reasons explain this.

Case study 4: Ethnic minorities

Despite having lived in Britain for 35 years, a 65-year-old Bangladeshi man had a remarkably poor understanding of British financial services provision. The only financial institutions he was aware of were banks, and the only financial product he had ever had was a savings account that was no longer in use. He described banks as 'very fussy', adding that there was a lot of paperwork, requiring so much personal information and checks of identification, that he did not want to open an account with them.

He preferred to rely on family and friends if they needed to borrow money or to replace possessions following a burglary. He also looked to his children to provide for him and his wife in their old age.

First, some people face language problems and difficulties with the paperwork required when applying for financial products. Among some groups, there is poor understanding of financial services in Britain, including what is available as well as how to get it. For followers of Islam, use of financial services is limited for religious reasons. Finally, there is, among some ethnic minorities, a cultural tradition of relying on the extended family network rather than using commercial sources of finance.

Combined, these reasons almost certainly explain why Pakistani and Bangladeshi households are more likely to be without financial products than are white households in similar socioeconomic circumstances (see Chapter 2). In contrast, other minority groups – such as African-Caribbeans – are more likely to lack financial products because they are on the margins of the labour market or are single mothers. This, too, is consistent with the results of the modelling reported in Chapter 2.

Disengagement from financial services

About a quarter of households with no financial products have in fact used them in the past, but have given them up. These split about evenly into those who have experienced a substantial drop in income and women who have been left without financial products following separation or divorce or the death of their partner. A minority of people in these circumstances are either refused products outright or have facilities withdrawn; most of them disengage because the products on offer are felt to be inappropriate or too costly for someone living on a very low income. The fact that state benefits and pensions can be drawn in cash seems to further encourage people to operate a cash budget, a finding consistent with the statistical modelling reported in Chapter 2.

Disengagement following a drop in income

Many people decide to stop using financial services when they have experienced a drop in income, some because they want to keep control over their money, others because they get into financial difficulties.

Disengagement to keep financial control

When the main wage earner loses their job, households typically re-appraise their financial situation. For some this is an immediate response as they attempt to accommodate levels of committed expenditure within a drastically reduced budget. A similar process of disengagement occurs when the main, or sole, wage earner is unable to work through ill-health or disability.

Case study 5: Disengagement following unemployment

A couple in their 40s had been dependent on state benefits since the husband was made redundant. They had progressively opted out of using financial services, suspending use of their current account and collecting benefit money in cash to keep a close eye on their budget. They had cashed in a life insurance policy because they could not afford to keep up the payments, and felt that use of high street consumer credit was inappropriate in their present economic circumstances. They had, however, recently taken out a loan with a weekly collected credit company. Because they could make small weekly cash payments, they felt they were much less likely to fall into arrears, and it enabled them to keep their borrowing under control.

Depending on their incomes, some people give up financial products following retirement, although this is a more gradual process of disengagement than for either the unemployed or long-term sick or disabled. Women often suspend or close financial products when they give up work to have children. In cases where the woman has a partner, the household relies on financial products in his name. Single mothers, however, do not have this option and many choose to disengage from financial services when they leave work and start to claim Income Support. Disengagement also occurs following relationship breakdown, when women who have been accustomed to a reasonable standard of living have to manage on a greatly reduced income.

Case study 6: Disengagement following retirement

A couple in their late 60s had altered their whole way of managing money since retiring to suit their reduced income. They had stopped using almost all financial products, including their current account, and had only retained a building society savings account, which they used to raise cheques when necessary. "We haven't got a bank account, we don't pay anything direct debit. When you live on a pension, you've got to do it, sort of pay week by week because you've only got a basic pension to live on."

Among all these people, there is a clear feeling that financial services are really only appropriate while in work. They deploy a range of strategies to keep control of their budget that result in a gradual disengagement from financial services.

Their first strategy for making ends meet is to run down any available savings. Some close down their savings accounts; others retain a very small amount of money in them, but generally this is no more than a few pounds.

Next, they either let life insurance policies lapse or cash them in, or they fail to renew annual policies, such as house and contents insurance. Faced with a need to re-balance the household budget, insurance policies are thought of as an unaffordable luxury. The only exception to this is life insurance for children, which parents try to retain, if at all possible.

At the same time they stop using commercial credit, and other credit facilities such as hire purchase are paid off and not replaced. Some households begin using moneylenders (weekly collected credit) or borrow from the Social Fund if they are eligible. These one-off loans give them greater control over their spending than either overdrafts or credit cards. And because the repayments are either collected weekly or deducted from benefit payments, they are less likely to fall into arrears.

Finally, they suspend the use of their current account and may close it altogether. On the whole, bank accounts are seen as useful for their associated facilities – standing orders, direct debits, overdraft facilities, cheque books and debit cards. But there is a strong feeling among this group that it is too easy to lose control if these facilities are used. Without them, the account is of such limited use that they cease to use it altogether.

The process of disengagement takes differing lengths of time, depending on the event that precipitates the drop in income. On the whole, it is slowest for those who retire, where the drop in income is usually anticipated and occurs at a stage in the life cycle when demands on the household budget are probably at their minimum. People giving up work because of sickness or disability, who do not expect to return to full-time employment, are generally the quickest to disengage.

Disengagement in response to financial difficulties

Disengagement in response to financial difficulties occurs in broadly similar circumstances, although it is much less common following retirement. It tends to occur among households that experience a sudden drop in income and are left with financial commitments that cannot be met. In contrast to those who disengage to keep financial control, rather than immediately closing down financial products,

these people begin to juggle their financial affairs, typically 'robbing Peter to pay Paul' and relying on credit to see them through. They often have no savings (or redundancy/ retirement lump sums) to mitigate the transition to a low income.

In contrast to those who want to keep control, the process of disengagement for households who are in financial difficulty is often imposed through an inability to keep up payments, and usually occurs at a later stage. The strategies employed by this group in order to regain control over their budget are also somewhat different.

Case study 7: Disengagement following financial difficulties

A 50-year-old couple fell into financial difficulties when the husband became unable to work five years ago. When the wife was made redundant two-and-a-half years later, she tried to claim on an insurance policy to cover the repayments on a loan. This was only successful on appeal, by which time they owed money to a number of creditors and had been borrowing from a weekly collected credit company to make ends meet – even this company now refused them further credit. During this time, they had overdrawn their current account by £3 and incurred £38 bank charges. They had since stopped using the account entirely.

"I don't use it because I can't get a loan or an overdraft and I don't have anything to put into my bank. I have a cheque book and a cheque guarantee card but, as I said, I don't use them."

As they are quite unlikely to have any savings, households in this group more typically rely on overdraft facilities and credit cards to make ends meet during the initial period following the income reduction.

In some cases, current accounts and credit facilities are withdrawn, in others charges imposed for unauthorised overdrafts or missed credit payments lead to closure/suspension of current accounts and of credit facilities. Having a history of debt makes it difficult for this group of people to regain access to many financial products.

Disengagement following relationship breakdown or widowhood

As well as income-related disengagement following relationship breakdown discussed above, women may also find themselves without access to financial services facilities following separation, divorce or the death of a partner. These comprise two main groups: women who cannot get financial products in their own right, and those who do not want to use them.

Left without facilities and cannot get them

Typically, this group comprises divorced or separated women who previously used all financial products in their husband's name alone, or in joint names. After separation, they need to take out new financial services in their own right. While those in full-time work usually face no problems doing so, women who care for their children full-time and rely on Income Support for their income may find that they are denied access to financial services. They are often rehoused on hard-to-let estates and this, together with their economic circumstances, can act as a barrier to accessing financial services. Those whose marriages end with money owed to creditors have the hardest time of all.

Case study 8: Disengagement following relationship breakdown and cannot get facilities

A young mother had recently separated from her husband when their house was repossessed. When married, as well as a mortgage they had had buildings and home contents insurance and had used a variety of credit sources. Following separation, she was rehoused on a hard-to-let council estate where she could no longer afford to insure her possessions. She could not get access to credit, nor could she get a current account in her own name. In fact, she was a very careful money manager and her husband had got them into financial difficulties.

Left without facilities and do not want them

These women are left without financial products in similar circumstances, although they include more women whose partner has died, often leaving them to manage on a low income.

Case study 9: Disengagement following relationship breakdown and does not want facilities

A woman in her 60s had not worked for 12 years because of ill-health. Consequently, when she separated from her husband, almost all financial products were in his name. She decided against taking out replacement products due to her drop in income. She felt that a cash budget gave her far greater control – she drew her pension weekly in cash and made weekly payments towards all her bills there and then. The remaining money she managed on a daily basis.

They differ from the previous group in that they *choose* not to take on financial products in their own name, because they prefer to manage their household budget in cash. Often they are women who have previously played only a minor role in household money management.

Individuals within households

So far we have concentrated on *households* with little or no use of financial services, on the grounds that many products are best viewed in that way. A home contents insurance policy, for example, covers all members of a household. But it is important to acknowledge that individuals within a household may not have products personally even though someone else may have them. The most common situation is among women, who rely on financial products, including current and savings accounts, that are held in their partner's name.

Some will have had them in the past, but given them up. This is most common among women who give up work to raise a family and have a partner who manages all the household finances and has all the financial products needed by the household in his name.

Others will never have had financial products in their own name. The two most common cases are elderly women who have not worked since having children and women from some ethnic minority groups (Pakistani and Bangladeshi women in particular), where the cultural division of responsibilities means that women neither take paid employment nor do they play a part in managing the household finances.

For the most part it is unproblematic for the individuals concerned to rely on someone else's bank account or other financial products, unless the relationship breaks down or the partner dies, in which case women can be left with no products at all, as just described. The other instance when it is highly problematic is in violent relationships, when keeping control of the household finances is part and parcel of the mental pressure exerted by violent partners.

Engagement and re-engagement with financial services

So far, we have concentrated on the reasons why some people are marginalised from financial services provision. The other side of the same coin is to gain an understanding of why people start using financial products in the first place and, in particular, the circumstances that lead disengaged users to start re-using them.

Using financial products for the first time

Most people start to use financial products while they are still relatively young – especially if their parents are, themselves, financial service users. Typically, they begin by opening a savings account, followed by a current account into which wages can be paid when they gain secure employment.

Once people have 'put a toe in the water' of financial services they commonly receive marketing material offering them other products. As they move into independent adult life, getting a home of their own, and especially when setting up home with a partner, they increase the range of financial products they use to include insurance and more sophisticated savings products. Indeed, rising home ownership will have played an important part in the increased use of financial services.

Clearly, then, most young people become engaged with financial services at some stage in their lives. The factors that inhibit this include:

- being unable to get a foothold in the labour market because of an unstable work history, single parenthood, or ill-health or disability;

- having parents who do not use financial services;

- living in a marginalised community.

The process of re-engagement

Some of those who disengage will probably remain non-users of financial services for considerable periods of time – maybe for the rest of their life. This is especially so for those who retire or do not expect to work again because of ill-health or disability. It is also the case for unemployed people in late middle-age who are not hopeful of finding work before they retire.

For others, there will come a time when they re-engage with financial services, usually when they return to work. On the whole, this re-engagement is a gradual process. The households that initially disengaged to keep in control remain cautious for some time after returning to employment, while those forced to disengage through financial difficulties face an even longer re-engagement process – not only are they left with a legacy of financial problems but they commonly find that access to current accounts and credit is restricted by their history of debt.

Case study 10: The process of re-engagement

A couple, both aged 38, had disengaged from all financial services, including life and medical insurance policies, while the husband was unable to work because of ill-health; they had accrued debts amounting to over £5,000 which were being repaid through a court Administration Order.

When the husband returned to work, they opened a building society current account into which his wages were paid and which they also used to pay their bills by standing order. They decided against having a cheque book as "it's too much of a temptation – we use his mum's cheque book if we need a cheque". They had also taken a new home contents insurance policy, but had an indemnity (second-hand replacement) rather than a 'new for old' policy because it was cheaper.

Exclusion or self-exclusion?

This analysis raises the question, are people excluded or do they self-exclude? At the extremes the answer is straightforward. A small minority are denied access to individual financial products; and, equally, a small minority have quite clearly decided not to use them (Table 3.1).

Table 3.1: Exclusion and self-exclusion from financial products

cell percentages

	% of all households who lack individual products
Exclusion*	
Current account	
Withdrawn by bank/building society	4
Refused by bank/building society	2
Consumer credit	
No one will offer it to me	4
Home contents insurance	
Applied and was turned down	1
Self-exclusion	
Current account	
Prefer cash**	28
Consumer credit	
Opposed to borrowing	26
Home contents insurance	
Object on principle	2

Source: *Office of Fair Trading* (1999). Base: current account 298; consumer credit 1,036; home contents insurance 566.

* These percentages are of households who say they do not have access at all because they have been refused. Many more households will have been refused by one or more companies, but been able to find a supplier. For example, the Office of Fair Trading found that individual banks refuse between 13 and 41% of applications for a current account.

** The depth interviews show that this overstates the degree of self-exclusion, as many people prefer cash because a current account gives them too little control.

But between these extremes is a grey area where people face barriers that encourage self-exclusion. First, households are deterred by price considerations. This applies to low pay-outs if life insurance policies are surrendered in the first few years; the very high cost of credit sources available to people on low incomes; the charges incurred by inadvertently overdrawing a current account; and unaffordable insurance premiums. As one candid insurer commented, "There is no such thing as an uninsurable household, merely an unaffordable premium". In other words, there is *price exclusion*.

Second, households are deterred by the conditions attached to financial products – *condition exclusion*. These include being offered insurance policies with high excesses or containing exclusions that severely limit the policy's usefulness (although it may reduce its cost). They also include current accounts which are offered with very limited facilities – no cheque book or cheque guarantee card, for example – and current accounts where charges are imposed for very short-term overdrawing by small amounts. Finally, they include life insurance policies which, if payment is not maintained, have, under current legislation, to be lapsed.

Third, there is *marketing exclusion*. Households who have never really used financial services typically receive few approaches to try and sell them financial products. The Office of Fair Trading data on vulnerable consumers, for example, shows that 64% of households with no financial products had had no sales approaches in the past year. This compares with 20% of households that were using financial services. Consequently, as the depth interviews showed all too graphically, many have very little knowledge of financial products or how to go about getting them.

Rarely, though, is the situation clear-cut. Most people who have no, or very few, financial products are affected by all these processes to some degree. Moreover, while very few cited the lack of financial service outlets as the main reason for not having particular products (only 1% of households without a current account said it was because there was no local branch), it was clear from the focus groups that limited geographical access leads to a considerable psychological barrier. The feeling that financial services are not for households on very low incomes was similarly very widespread.

Note

[1] This estimate is based on data collected from the Office of Fair Trading (1999).

4

Unmet needs and the consequences of financial exclusion

Financial exclusion is not a new problem – there has always been a group of people without access to a wide range of financial products – and, in fact, it now affects a smaller proportion of households than used to be the case (Berthoud and Kempson, 1992; Kempson, 1994; Whyley et al, 1998). However, the consequences of not having access to key financial products – a bank account, consumer credit, savings, or insurance – are much more serious now than they were in the past. Being part of a small minority who are outside mainstream financial services creates a new set of difficulties. On the whole, the options for operating a household budget outside the mainstream financial services sector are far more costly and often unregulated. Moreover, where whole communities have limited access to financial products, the process becomes self-reinforcing and an important contributor to social exclusion more generally.

One of the most important findings from the focus groups is that there clearly *is* a need for financial products among people who make little or no use of financial services. Moreover, these needs are both practical and functional. Broadly, there are two main types of unmet needs: for financial products to assist day-to-day money management and financial transactions and for long-term financial security (Table 4.1). In contrast, there was little expressed need for savings or consumer credit products to assist with the purchase of consumer goods.

Day-to-day money management

Altogether over a third of all the focus group participants identified some aspect of day-to-day money management as their top priority and about a third gave it as a second priority. For the most part, this was having somewhere to have wages or benefits paid into, although a minority said they needed other types of facility. Subsequent discussion, however, uncovered more widespread needs for a means of bill payment and short-term credit to make ends meet.

The reasons for these priorities were not hard to find. For those households without a current account, financial transactions, notably bill payment and cheque handling, become a great deal more complicated. Although most people (in both the focus groups and the depth interviews) who lacked a current account had decided not to use one so they could keep close control over their money, the methods they had devised for a cash budget were time-consuming, involved charges and often meant they paid more for basic household services. Similarly, not having access to short-term credit to smooth the peaks and troughs of household finances at best complicates budgeting, and at worst results in arrears or the use of high-cost moneylenders.

A current account

This was the most common need in the focus groups, with many people saying their priority was for somewhere to have wages paid in, often in combination with having a place to keep money until needed. On the whole, these priorities were of equal importance for men and women and they were most often expressed by younger people, for whom bank or building society accounts are the accepted way of dealing with daily financial transactions.

Table 4.1: Priorities for financial products

	1st priority	2nd priority	Lowest priority*
			absolute numbers
Day-to-day money management	**12**	**9**	**4**
Somewhere to have wages or benefits paid into	9	1	1
Somewhere to keep money until ready to spend it	2	4	1
A way of cashing/issuing cheques	1	1	1
Short-term credit to make ends meet	0	2	0
A means of automatic bill-payment	0	1	1
Long-term financial security	**11**	**18**	**5**
Providing for your family in case something happens	7	5	2
Providing for old age	4	7	2
Setting aside money for children's future	0	6	1
Medium-term financial security	**8**	**2**	**2**
Insurance against job loss	6	0	2
Replacing lost or damaged household items	2	2	0
Purchasing consumer goods	**0**	**2**	**18**
Longer-term credit for more expensive items	0	1	9
Saving up for expensive items	0	1	9

* No information for three respondents.

Note: At the start of each group, participants were given a list of 12 key functions for which financial products are used. Functions were used instead of the names of actual products to discourage people from thinking only in terms of products which are currently available and encourage a more creative perspective. Each person was asked to select their first priority, second priority and lowest priority. These could include something for which they were already using financial products.

Needing somewhere to have income paid in was most important for people aged under 45 and was usually associated with wages rather than social security benefit income. All were in work or hoped to be soon and virtually everyone who gave it a high priority believed that a current account was essential for anyone in employment, as they believed that wages could only be paid via a bank account.

"If I don't have an account, I can't get paid."

"... everybody needs that if they've got wages coming, you need a bank account."

Likewise, needing somewhere to keep money was also associated with having an earned income. All who gave this as a priority either had an earned income or they (or their partner) were looking for work. But they needed an account as a means of money management rather than as a formal, regular savings product. They were mostly aged under 35 and were more likely not to have financial products *yet* rather than to be on the margins of financial

services. Several of them were new householders setting up home who needed to buy more expensive household items and, therefore, having somewhere to keep money where they would not be tempted to spend it was important.

On the whole, the people who needed these facilities tended to have them. This was confirmed by a recent study of access to current accounts, although it also found that one in five of households lacking a current account said they needed somewhere to have their income paid in and one in six wanted somewhere to keep money (Kempson and Whyley, 1998).

Bill payment

Although bill payment was not initially identified as a priority by many people in the focus groups, it cropped up frequently as a problem in the everyday lives both of the group participants and the depth interviews[1].

Payment of household bills now relies heavily on having access to a bank or building society account and the majority of households pay their bills in this way. In contrast, people without a current account settle their bills in a variety of ways including paying in cash at Post Offices, using pay-as-you-go methods such as prepayment meters, or buying savings stamps. This is often built into a routine, with people making weekly payments and buying savings stamps when they draw their benefits or state pension at the Post Office and then going to the nearest outlet to charge up the keys for their prepayment meters.

Householders who pay their bills in cash manage their money in a variety of ways. Some set money aside towards quarterly bills using a variety of containers such as jars, boxes and envelopes – a separate container is allocated to a specific bill. They then take the cash to the nearest office where payment can be made. The risks of having large amounts of cash in the home are obvious. A number of the people interviewed in-depth for a study on home contents insurance, who did not have a current account, had bill money stolen from their homes.

Moreover, the options for spreading annual or quarterly bills are very limited for someone with no access to direct debit or standing order facilities. In addition, the number of outlets where bills can be settled in cash has been decreasing, although the recent establishment of the PayPoint service has begun to address this. PayPoint operates through a range of outlets – including corner shops and petrol stations – with the aim that everyone living in an urban area should have an outlet within one mile of their home; in rural areas it should be five miles.

Uppermost in most people's minds was the cost of paying bills without a current account. Paying bills in cash often incurs additional charges – up to £0.90 per transaction at the Post Office. In addition, some creditors, such as the utility companies, now offer large discounts to customers settling their accounts by direct debit, so that people paying in cash effectively pay a higher tariff. Prepayment fuel customers pay an even higher tariff. A recent study of competition in the gas industry found that not being able to pay bills by direct debit meant paying up to £46 more a year on an average gas bill (Whyley and Kempson, 1998). Moreover, settling bills fortnightly in cash could incur additional handling charges of up to £24 a year

(£48 if paid weekly), while prepayment meter customers could pay as much as £80 a year more on average levels of use.

Above all, paying bills in cash is very time-consuming – many of the focus group participants would have welcomed some way of reducing the time and worry involved in making sure all bills were up-to-date. Two lone parents discussed the value of Fuel Direct, a system designed to help benefit claimants clear arrears with utility bills by making direct deductions from their benefit entitlement and passing it on to their creditors. This system not only gave them the security of knowing their bills were paid, but also took some of the pressures of money management out of their hands.

"It's like the social. They'll pay your bills for you ... they'll take it out for you and you get used to that, it's peace of mind – your bills are being paid. But when you've got to go down the Post Office [and think] 'Shall I pay that bill or shall I go and do this?'"

"... something else might crop up. You know you've got to pay that £20 electric, but something might crop up, like it's one of the kid's birthdays or something, and you haven't really got a lot of money ... so the electric goes out of the way because your priority is your kids, and next week it's £40."

Direct debits would not meet their needs for two important reasons. First, as noted above, direct debits are paid monthly while most of these households prefer to operate weekly or fortnightly budgets. Second, they feared loss of control over their money. A remarkably high proportion of people in both the focus groups and the depth interviews either had personal experience of accounts becoming overdrawn through the timing of payments in and out, or they had known friends or relatives get into that position.

There are some companies that specialise in handling the bill payments from households dealing in cash. They collect a regular amount from the customer's home and, if there is insufficient in the account to pay all bills, advance cash loans to cover the payments. Such services are not, however, without problems. A pensioner couple had used such a company for 25 years, and currently paid £25 a week. They had no idea how much of this was a charge for the service and how much went towards their bills. Nor did they know what rate of interest they were charged if the 'account' went overdrawn.

The real need was for a simple current account, from which bills could be paid in regular, agreed weekly or fortnightly amounts, with no overdraft facility, but a 'buffer zone' permitting overdrawing by small amounts for up to a week without incurring charges. This is explored in more detail in the following chapter.

Handling cheques

Receiving or needing to issue a cheque is quite a problem for people who lack either a current or a savings account. Since the introduction of the 1992 Cheques Act, all cheques are crossed 'a/c payee only', so people without a current account have difficulties handling them. Indeed, the receipt of a cheque was often the trigger for opening an account, as was getting a wage. The number of employers willing to pay wages in cash has declined significantly since the repeal of the Truck Acts.

On the whole, handling cheques was not a major problem for households lacking a current account – only one in 10 identified it as an unmet need in a recent study of access to current accounts (Kempson and Whyley, 1998). The focus groups and depth interviews showed that people lacking an account either had cheques made out in a relative's name or paid them into a relative's account and asked them to give them cash.

> "My housing benefit is paid directly to me, but usually you can sign the back and get it cashed by someone else. But now they're changing the rules where it's got to go into a bank account ... my rent is now sent off monthly by my brother's cheque and he gives me the money.... These money people who cash cheques will not cash a housing benefit cheque."

In fact, there is a new, and rapidly growing, network of cheque cashers (set up following the 1992 Act) which enable people without

accounts to cash most cheques. The fee for this service is typically between 7 and 9% of the value of the cheque, plus a flat fee of £2.

Where people needed to issue cheques they generally 'bought' one from a relative or friend with an account. This was remarkably common and took several forms. Some people saved up cash and then asked for a cheque; one woman actually saved towards her bills using her friend's account and asked for a cheque when she received the bill; others would ask a relative to write out a cheque and then pay off the 'debt'.

Short-term credit to help make ends meet

In general, there was a good deal of resistance to the use of credit among the focus group participants. But this was usually coupled with a realisation that there are times when it is necessary to smooth the peaks and troughs that occur in household budgets. Consequently, people with no overdraft facility or credit card have to find other ways of making ends meet.

Households on a low income regularly help one another out at the end of the week or fortnight. Mothers and daughters, sisters and even close female friends often have such reciprocal lending arrangements involving goods or small amounts of cash.

Few, however, have someone they can turn to for larger sums in an emergency – such as an unexpectedly high bill. People in these circumstances often have little choice but to use moneylenders or pawnbrokers and, consequently, to pay their high charges. Several had lost valuables in this way, such as one woman who had pawned jewellery valued at £200 for a £50 loan to pay bills and been unable to redeem it. In her view, pawnbrokers are "... right cons. They don't give you much for your stuff, they rob you".

It was relatively common for households to use licensed moneylenders, paying between 100 and 500% APRs, depending on the size and length of the loan. One family had taken out a £60 loan for 20 weeks, which was being repaid at £4.20 a week – a total 'interest'[2] payment of £24; a lone mother had borrowed £200, which was to be repaid at £6.80 a week for 50 weeks, putting the 'interest' at £140.

Some households, however, do not even have this option open to them, largely because of where they live, as licensed companies, quite understandably, are unwilling to send collectors (who carry large amounts of cash) on to high-crime estates. People living on these estates may then turn to unlicensed lenders who charge extortionate rates of interest. A lone parent living on a notorious South London council estate, for example, borrowed £50 for a month and had to pay back £10 'interest'; a pensioner couple had paid £250 'interest' on a £500 loan for 20 weeks.

Worse still, some lenders engage in illegal practices to encourage payment, such as taking benefit books or passports as 'security' for the loan. A Bangladeshi man had needed to borrow money in an emergency and had no choice but to use an unlicensed lender from within his community.

> "I had to leave my passport with him as security ... he would turn up the day before the payment was due and remind me that if I missed the payment then I would have to pay him £200. He was not very compassionate and even when I paid it all off he delayed giving my passport back."

In some Asian communities there are also 'go-betweens' who, for a fee, will help people apply for financial services. These seem to operate in different ways. On the one hand, some act almost like brokers, fixing up credit agreements for people with poor English and little knowledge of British financial services. Fees vary according to the size of the loan. But there is a second kind of go-between, who arranges loans and handles the repayments. The borderline between this and moneylending is a fine one. Neither type is registered and so the practice is entirely unregulated.

Longer-term financial security

The need for longer-term financial security was paramount for around a third of people who took part in the focus groups, while even more said it was their second priority. A central factor in the depth and breadth of this need were the strong feelings of insecurity expressed by many people in the groups and, for some, a

recognition that circumstances were unlikely to change in the near future. Consequently, many of them felt that they had no 'safety net' and this was a source of great concern.

Householders with dependent children were especially likely to say they wanted to be able to provide financial security for their family; older people wanted to be able to provide for themselves in their old age.

Security for families and children

Discussions on providing financial security for families centred around two areas:

- ensuring that families were provided for should anything happen to the main carer and/or wage earner;

- putting money aside for children's future.

For many people, both of these functions were important but, of the two, being able to save money towards a child's future was clearly secondary to the peace of mind of knowing they would be looked after if anything should happen.

Providing financial security for their family was most important to women and, not surprisingly, to lone parents in particular. Mothers felt that providing a 'safety net' for their children was the least they could do as they felt they could not rely on the State to provide adequately for their children.

> "I'm a one parent family and if I can't do anything else, at least that's what I'd like to be able to do, is to provide for them."

People made a clear distinction between a financial safety net and setting money aside to give to children in the future. While six of the 31 people in the focus groups identified this as an important need, it was never a top priority. Although most parents expressed a desire to give their children a 'good start' and to be able to offer them financial help when they needed it, this was clearly not perceived to be as fundamentally important as ensuring they were provided for should something happen to their parent. These two forms of security for families were, however, closely linked in people's minds.

Again, people who identified a need for a way of saving for their children were mostly lone parents who felt a responsibility to provide their children with financial security and independence for the future.

> "When they get to, say 18, they get a decent lump sum, so it gives you a bit of peace of mind of knowing they've got that to fall back on as well ... something for when they get older, something to give them a wee pick-up. Oh yeah, it gives you good peace of mind knowing that they've got a bit of a start when they get to adulthood."

Security for old age

The issue of financial provision for old age was clearly of concern to a significant proportion of people in the focus groups. Around a third of them accorded it either first or, more commonly, second priority.

Not surprisingly it was of greatest importance to people who were already retired or approaching retirement, and without any savings or provision for their old age. Crucially, however, it was most important to people whose children were no longer dependent on them. There was a clear hierarchy of need whereby children's needs were taken care of first and, only when children became independent, did parents turn their minds to their own financial security.

There was a widespread belief that it was unrealistic to expect the State pension to provide an adequate income in old age. Indeed, some younger people doubted whether there would be one at all by the time they retired.

As we have already seen, retiring to live on a very low income can lead people to a more general disengagement from financial services – running down such savings as they have, letting insurance policies lapse through lack of money, and closing down credit facilities and current accounts.

It also has a direct effect on their standard of living. People with no personal or occupational pension provision, who are solely dependent on the State pension in retirement, face a struggle to make ends meet.

> "Speaking personally, you think, when you retire, that you're going to be well off in your old age, but the way circumstances are financially and politically, you finish up being very poor."

> "I wasn't even left comfortable when my husband died, I had to pay off his bills, so I have to rely on my [State] pension and that's it."

Divorced women who currently lose their rights to their husband's occupational pension, particularly suffer from the lack of a private pension as they often experience a very large drop in income if they divorce just before retirement.

Most pensioners in this position are determined to live within their means, which necessitates making difficult decisions about spending priorities. Many cut down on food or use of fuel to keep within their budget. It can also mean falling into arrears with bills or relying on moneylenders to make ends meet. Younger participants in the focus groups were agreed that, if they reached pension age with no private pension, they would have no option but to keep on working.

Medium–term financial security

Although most needs identified in the focus groups related to either day-to-day money management or long-term financial security, a smaller group of people were worried about more medium-term needs. This included both insurance against job loss and, to a lesser degree, home contents insurance.

Insurance against job loss

Being able to protect themselves against the loss of earned income was surprisingly important to people in the focus groups, particularly given the low incidence of paid employment among them. Just one of the six focus group participants who identified this as their top priority was in work and this was only part-time. All of them were the only potential wage earners in their household and expressed an awareness that there were 'no jobs for life'.

Some were young men who had hardly been in the labour market, if at all, since they left school. Others were women who were unable to work due to caring responsibilities and did not expect to be able to join the workforce for some years to come.

They were well aware, from personal experience, of the inadequacy of State benefits and the financial stringencies they impose. Consequently, if they ever did find paid work, they wanted to protect themselves from being catapulted back into the same circumstances in the future.

There is, however, clear evidence that those with unstable work histories or a history of ill-health are the least likely to have (and to be able to get) insurance to cover them in case they should lose their job through redundancy or ill-health. And, where they *are* able to get a policy it often contains clauses that mean they do not actually receive any payments when they become unable to work (Ford and Kempson, 1997; Kempson et al, 1999: forthcoming).

Home contents insurance

For many people living on a low income, home contents insurance is a luxury they cannot afford. A minority of participants in the focus groups, however, did identify it as one of their priority needs. This was largely based on their concerns about the potential consequences of being uninsured.

Previous research has shown that one in six households with no home contents insurance had experienced a burglary or, less commonly, a fire or flood. Indeed, people living on vandalised housing estates with high levels of crime are unlikely to be able to afford a home contents insurance policy, simply because they *are* very likely to be burgled (Whyley et al, 1998).

Moreover, compared with their insured counterparts who had lost possessions, those who had no policy to draw on were much less secure financially. Two thirds of them had no savings at all, more than half had household incomes below £100 a week, and half of them said they were experiencing financial difficulties. They were also likely to lose necessities rather than luxury goods, yet over half of them were unable to replace the items they had lost.

For example, a lone mother could not afford home contents insurance because she lived on a high-crime estate. When she was burgled she lost her television and jewellery, which she could not afford to replace, but described as "only possessions". Far worse was the fact that they took her benefit books as well.

> "Well they [Benefits Agency] wouldn't replace them, believe it or not, 'we can't help you'. I put in for a crisis loan on the same day, they wouldn't help us there, they said 'No, it's been cashed'. I thought, well how can that be...."

She sought help from her local citizen's advice bureau and eventually the matter was sorted out. Meanwhile,

> "I had to borrow and borrow for a full week until my money was due the next Monday and by that time you were knocked off balance anyhow, it knocked you to hell for, as I say, about four weeks."

Purchasing consumer goods

Two thirds of people in the groups said their lowest priority, as regards financial services, was either longer-term loans or way of saving up for expensive items. Indeed, there was a wholesale rejection of 'expensive items' as being quite inappropriate in their circumstances:

> "Well, you're usually trying to sort out the rest of your bills and everything else, and you don't usually have enough at the end of the day to say, 'Well, that's been put away for a £1,000 three piece suite', because half the time little Joe wants a new pair of shoes, or big Katie wants a brand new coat. So you don't have the money at the end of the day to say, 'Right, I'm putting £20 away for ...' you just can't do it."

Many of the households interviewed in-depth, that lacked formal savings products, did, nevertheless, save, although they did so informally. This included saving loose change in jars, buying savings stamps, paying into Christmas clubs, over-feeding prepayment meters to get a cash rebate, letting State benefits (normally Child Benefit) mount up before claiming them and giving small sums to a relative to hold for them. They saved for a number of purposes – for Christmas, to buy more expensive essentials and, where possible, for days out or a holiday. Above all they saved to meet their children's needs (see also Kempson, 1998).

In the focus groups, there was quite a strong, moral opposition to borrowing:

> "I was brought up that loans were definitely out. If you can't pay your way, you do without it and that's it."

And an awareness that, in their circumstances "credit means debt". Borrowing was not seen as a solution to their problems but as being likely to exacerbate them.

> "Because when I was 18 I had a £500 bank loan out ... but I went and had another loan and then I had a £1,000

loan ... and then I found it really hard paying it back, because I used to have to pay £100 a month back."

Despite this opposition, people with limited access to financial products often face difficulties accommodating 'lumpy' items of expenditure within a tight household budget. Buying or replacing household goods and buying more expensive items of clothing were the main examples quoted in both the focus groups and depth interviews. Those lacking access to high street credit had two choices. Some had used door-to-door moneylenders at very high rates of interest, others used credit through a third party – usually putting it in the name of a relative.

Notes

[1] It is possible that the wording used in the list prevented people selecting it, as *automatic* payment methods were not necessarily a high priority. What they did need, however, was a simple, cost-free method of paying bills in small, regular amounts.

[2] This does, in fact, include charges for door-to-door collection as well as the interest on the loan.

5

Meeting the needs of financially excluded households

All the evidence suggests that meeting the needs of households that currently lack financial products is not necessarily an insurmountable problem. On the whole, their requirements are not so very different from those of most other consumers. Where there are differences, these generally require fairly minor adjustments to existing products rather than fundamentally different forms of provision. Nor is there much appetite for dealing with alternative providers, who specialise in the needs of low-income households.

Essentially combating financial exclusion boils down to widening access, so that low-income households feel *in*cluded in financial services provision. This requires: providers who low-income households perceive to be accessible, both physically and psychologically; the availability of products that are appropriately designed for their needs; and the ability to make use of them through appropriate delivery mechanisms.

Providers of financial services

People who took part in the focus groups all wanted to deal with organisations that were reliable and financially secure. They indicated a strong desire to move away from alternative financial services and into mainstream provision.

> "It's got to be a reputable place, that's not going to go bust next week…. And it's got to be somewhere you can trust and you know that your money's going to be there when you need it at the end of the day."

Many also favoured 'household names', "big names, that's what you're looking for".

Just as importantly, they wanted to deal with organisations that they felt understood the financial circumstances of low-income households and who they perceived to be trustworthy. Several people in the focus groups felt that they were particularly vulnerable to exploitation by financial institutions. This view was largely the result of inappropriate marketing, which meant that the only financial products they were actively encouraged to take out were loans – often from non-mainstream providers at high costs. Further, they were most likely to be encouraged to borrow money when they were already paying off a loan, even if they were already experiencing repayment problems. Several people were worried they would submit to this "indiscriminate lending", even against their better judgement, because they were so often short of money.

Finally, they wanted financial service providers to have a presence in their community.

F1:   "If it's local, you can get down there."

F2:   "And you can speak to them, that's the important part…."

M1:   "If it's local, you can work there, or go on your bike. If you've got a groan or a moan, you've got it there haven't you? You're not dealing with someone that's distant."

F1:   "But not only that, if there should be a problem, if you're going all the way [into town], you're just a number to them."

Note: F=female; M=male interviewee.

When asked to identify the financial services provider they would most like to deal with, the vast majority of people in all five focus groups named organisations with a local presence. In four cases, this was the local authority or Benefits Agency and none of the people in these groups lived in communities with locally-based financial service providers. The fifth group nominated the bank which still had a branch in their village, yet they were equally clear that they would not feel the same way about a bank located in the nearest large town, still less in the nearest city. In part, this was because of the costs and difficulties of getting to offices some distance from their home. More importantly, though, it was because they felt that more remote providers were not interested in having them as customers and would, in any case, have little understanding of their needs and circumstances.

Appropriate product design and delivery

During the course of the focus group, discussions participants identified a number of important requirements most of which apply to a broad range of financial products. We therefore begin by considering each of these requirements in turn before assessing the extent to which existing products are able to meet them.

In fact, many of the requirements identified in the focus groups are very similar to those of any consumer: simplicity and transparency; cost and value for money; and appropriate marketing. Others, such as the need for greater flexibility and appropriate delivery mechanisms, are particular to households on a low income. The participants recognised that, in some circumstances, these requirements were incompatible and that there would have to be trade-offs. It may also be the case that some needs cannot be met by the private sector alone and that public–private partnerships may be required.

Simplicity and transparency

On the whole, the focus group participants wanted financial products that would help them in their need to keep close control over their money. This generally meant products that

were simpler and more transparent than those currently available.

Simple, 'no frills' products were attractive because they could be used with confidence and would provide a relatively secure base from which people could become familiar with the financial services. At the same time, they would also go a long way towards achieving wider access to mainstream financial services as they would almost certainly require less stringent risk assessment.

Transparency was a key consideration because products that involve remote transactions, clauses which are difficult to understand or charging mechanisms that are hard to keep track of, all increase the risk of losing control over the household budget. The vast majority of people who use financial products want to be able to understand them and keep track of their money. For people who have not used financial products before and those with tight resources, however, the implications of making mistakes or losing track of the household budget can be much more serious.

Flexibility

The circumstances of low-income households are subject to frequent change. Consequently, as shown in Chapter 3, there is a high degree of churning in their use of financial products. The importance of flexibility lies in the extent to which financial products, particularly longer-term insurance and savings products, can adapt to these changes.

Low-income households need products with terms that can be altered should their circumstances change, to offer, for example, payment holidays or reduced payments for longer periods. They also need products which can be 'scaled down' to a minimum during times of hardship, when people need tight control over their spending. In addition, there was some support for using savings or insurance products as security for lower-cost credit facilities.

Appropriate delivery mechanisms

It is often assumed that low-income households simply cannot afford financial products like insurance, savings and credit, in any circumstances. Yet, the focus group discussions showed that it was not as simple as this and that some products cannot be afforded simply because mainstream products do not provide options for these households to pay in ways that can be accommodated within their household budget.

What most people wanted was the option of making small, frequent and regular payments for financial products. For the great majority this meant weekly or fortnightly, rather than monthly, payments. In addition, most people wanted to be able to establish a strict payment routine to reduce the likelihood of missing payments or spending the money on other things.

> "Because once it's in my hand it'd be difficult if I was wanting to buy something one week or if I was short one week, I might not pay it."

In the past, these requirements have been met by home service companies and a small number of people still preferred to do business in this way. But there was a strong feeling among the focus group participants that home service companies are "a thing of the past". Some people had also found that home service delivery had become much less reliable. Insurance agents did not call as frequently or as regularly as they had in the past, so breaking the discipline they felt was important. In addition, because fewer financial transactions are now conducted on the doorstep, home service delivery was felt to have become more stigmatised and was, therefore, less attractive to people who lived in smaller communities with a wide socioeconomic mix.

A large proportion of people in the focus groups felt that payment discipline was best induced by automatic cash transfer from their income.

> "I like fixed amounts, you know where you are, and I like it to come off at source from my wages."

> "I think you're reluctant to pay it when you've got to give it out of your hand into someone else's hand."

Although monthly direct debit facilities may have been accessible to those with current accounts, they did not entirely fulfil their needs. Many people were fearful of using them because of the danger of overdrawing and incurring financial penalties. Instead they would have preferred all payments for all or most of their regular commitments to be deducted from their income either at source or as soon as it is received into an account. This way they could be sure that their outgoings were covered and that any money left in their account was disposable income. In addition, direct debits can rarely be made on a weekly or fortnightly basis, and few people in the focus groups felt they could cope with monthly payments. What they wanted, ideally, was for the same set amount to be deducted from their income each week or fortnight (depending on their budgeting cycle).

Appropriate marketing

Despite the vast amount of promotional information about financial products that is received by most households, many people on low incomes are not sent any marketing literature at all. In part, this is likely to be because they are not using many, if any, financial products and are therefore not subject to attempts at cross-selling. It is also because increasingly precise geographical information systems facilitate highly specific targeting, so that marketing effort can be concentrated on the people which financial institutions most want to attract as customers.

This means that, as we saw in Chapter 4, low-income households are much less likely than people with higher incomes to receive marketing information about the products they need most, such as a basic bank or building society account. Conversely, where they do receive promotional literature, it tends to be for the products, such as credit and life insurance, which are least appropriate for people in their circumstances.

The impact of these patterns of marketing on low-income households is three-fold. First, it means they have very low levels of awareness about many mainstream financial products and how to obtain them. Second, it can generate a perception among low-income households that the kind of products they need most, such as a current account, are not available to people in their circumstances and that any attempt to obtain them would be unsuccessful. Third, it may encourage them into over-reliance on products which are not appropriate for their needs.

Cost and value for money

Generally speaking, focus group participants felt they paid more for, and got poorer returns from, financial services than other consumers.

A central question, however, is how appropriate financial products *could* be provided at a price which low-income households can afford. Clearly there will always be some financial products that are unaffordable on a low income, and some that will never be a spending priority for such households. In addition, meeting the specific needs of low-income households, and especially those relating to delivery, will inevitably cost more. Finally, reducing costs will not always result in better value for money. While recognising these points, the focus group participants raised some issues about cost and value for money which could be addressed.

First, the simpler mainstream financial products that group participants wanted would be cheaper to provide and to regulate and could, therefore, be made available at lower prices.

Second, cheaper products could also, in some instances, be achieved by breaking down complex financial products into smaller, more affordable parts. This would allow people who could not afford the product as a whole to buy the elements they felt they most needed. For example, some people were attracted to the idea of 'catastrophe only' home contents insurance, covering them against fire or flood but not burglary. However, experience in the insurance industry suggests that these products are generally unpopular. Further, while these unbundled products may be cheaper, they are also likely to represent poor value for money.

Conversely, offering low-income households the option of creating their own bundles of products could allow them to get each of these products at a lower price and at better value for money than if they bought them separately.

Third, creating delivery mechanisms which cater specifically to the needs of low-income

households will, in some circumstances, be expensive and could make it difficult for the industry to offer them products they could afford. The people who took part in the focus groups recognised this contradiction and did not expect the industry to bear all the additional costs involved in catering to their needs. Many low-income households are already accustomed to paying extra for delivery mechanisms such as pre-payment meters and doorstep credit facilities which are designed to fit in with their budgeting preferences.

Developments in information technology, however, offer considerable scope for reducing the costs of delivery. The move away from face-to-face and paper transactions should make it possible to design products that can be appropriately delivered to low-income households more cheaply than is currently the case.

Most people in the focus groups were, however, prepared to meet at least some of the additional costs involved in delivering appropriate financial products, providing the charges were perceived to be reasonable and not simply a way of increasing profits. This was, in fact, their main objection to using non-mainstream providers of financial services who they believed were simply making excessive profits as a result of their high charges.

How well do existing products match up to these criteria?

Although the requirements of low-income households are not drastically different from those of the great majority, most existing financial products fail to meet one or more of the criteria outlined above. In many cases, however, it is possible to identify relatively minor changes that would make them more appropriate to households who currently lack them. At the same time, it is important to remember that people in different circumstances have rather different priorities for financial services and that, even with the changes suggested, many people will decide not to make use of specific products. We are not advocating universal use of financial products, merely a widening of their availability.

Day-to-day money management

As the previous chapter showed in detail, the most common need among people in the focus groups was for a means of handling money on a day-to-day basis, including:

- somewhere into which income and cheques can be paid;

- somewhere money can be held until needed;

- a facility for spreading the cost of bills;

- but no revolving credit facilities.

Current accounts are most commonly used for such day-to-day money management but, in most instances, do not quite fit the needs of low-income households for two main reasons: the fact that they are normally linked to credit facilities and their lack of transparency.

Because just about all current accounts provide access to credit, in the form of unauthorised overdrafts, they are not freely available. With very few exceptions, applications for a current account are subject to credit scoring and, consequently, some people will be refused access to them. Moreover, money laundering regulations provide another potential hurdle for people with no permanent home address. Individual banks actually refuse between 13 and 41% of applications made to them (Office of Fair Trading, 1999). Many of these applicants will, eventually, be successful in getting an account elsewhere and recent research has found that only 2% of people lacking a current account said it was because they had been denied access entirely (Kempson and Whyley, 1998). However, credit scoring means that many of the people most likely to find access to a current account difficult will be refused access to cheque books, cheque guarantee cards, or debit cards. In fact, 10% of current account holders have no cheque book; 19% are without a cheque guarantee card; and 28% do not have a debit card (Kempson and Whyley, 1998).

Besides limited access to banking facilities, the fact that current accounts carry the possibility of unauthorised overdrawing also causes budgeting difficulties for households living on low incomes. Most of the focus group participants would have preferred not to be able to overdraw at all and for any credit they used

to be in the form of one-off credit agreements with fixed levels of repayment.

Equally, the lack of transparency which current accounts offer if they are used for money transactions is also a problem for low-income households, particularly when combined with the inflexibility of financial penalties for unauthorised overdrawing. Together these mean that these households are very vulnerable to incurring penalties for inadvertently overdrawing because the margins on their budgets are so tight. This results in what one young, single parent referred to as a "mad circle", whereby bank charges imposed an even greater strain on already tight budgets.

F1:   "Because I was charged for going a pound over…. The charges were something like £8, that's your standard charge isn't it, and then another £8 – all for going over."

F2:   "They charge you for every letter they send you, which is about £25."

F1:   "It was two days late that my money went into my bank."

The focus group participants stressed the importance of being able to work out, at any given time, which transactions have already been completed, which payments remain outstanding, and exactly how much money they have available. While the majority were adamant that they did not want access to any sort of revolving credit, such as an overdraft facility, they were keen on the idea of a 'buffer zone'. Being able to overdraw an account by a small amount of money, for a short period of time, without incurring charges could be extremely useful in helping low-income households to smooth their household budget and without forfeiting control over it.

The main alternative to a current account is a simple savings account which could overcome some of these problems. Low-income households will find it easier to gain access to a savings account, because they are not subject to credit-scoring. They are also simpler and have greater transparency. However, savings accounts do not provide access to as wide a range of functions as current accounts and may, therefore, still leave some needs unmet. More importantly, because some building society savings accounts require minimum deposits before an account can be opened, they may not, in practice, be available to low-income households. Further, at least one building society currently only allows one free withdrawal per week from accounts with balances of less than £500, any subsequent withdrawals are subject to a charge.

What low-income households actually need is a product which falls between a current account and a savings account, offering greater simplicity and transparency alongside a wider range of functions. Such products are beginning to come onto the market but these are not generally marketed to low-income households.

These simple current accounts do not, however, currently meet low-income households' needs for bill payment facilities. Many focus group participants wanted a means of spreading bills into equal weekly or fortnightly , preferably deducted directly from their income. This does not necessarily mean that creditors must accept payments of this frequency. The same end could be reached if people were able to transfer money into a linked, bill payment account on a regular basis. Payments could then be made, in full, to creditors at the end of the billing period. Access to an account such as this would simply mean that people could make payments towards their bills on a frequent, regular basis, in amounts they can afford. This sort of 'budgeting account' used to exist, but has come to be replaced by direct debits. Focus group participants recognised that they would need to pay for a facility such as this, but most were prepared to do so. They are, after all, accustomed to being charged for using facilities such as pre-payment meters.

So far, we have concentrated on the design of suitable accounts for day-to-day money management. There is also a potential problem of delivery. The focus groups indicate that high street banks and building societies are only perceived as able to meet the needs of low-income households where they have retained a local presence. Branch closures mean that some low-income households lack physical access to banks and building societies, particularly in rural areas and deprived communities (Leyshon and Thrift, 1995). Focus group participants who lived in areas where bank and building society branches had been

withdrawn drew attention to the costs of travelling to more distant facilities.

F1: "If you don't have transport, you're paying out money aren't you?"

F2: "Why pay a fiver to go into [town] just to put a tenner in?"

F3: "Why pay it on the bus just to go into [town] to put a tenner in an account?"

The introduction of new innovations such as telephone and computer banking are unlikely to overcome access problems for low-income households. First, because they are not generally targeted at this end of the market. More importantly, however, the Office of Fair Trading data shows that 40% of households without financial products do not have access to a telephone and 96% are without access to a computer. Likewise supermarket banking does not overcome physical access problems as these, too, are some distance from where people on low incomes live. And the cut-price supermarkets used by such households are not the ones offering banking facilities (Kempson, 1996).

The problems of physical access, however, may not be as significant as the psychological barriers which result from branch closures. The focus groups clearly emphasise that unless high street banks and building societies have a local presence in people's lives, they are not perceived to be interested in serving them and are therefore not uppermost in their minds when they think about potential providers of financial services. One way round these difficulties may be for current accounts to be accessible through local intermediaries (the local authority or credit unions, for example) in ways that are similar to the public–private partnerships that have been set up for increasing access to home contents insurance. These are described more fully below.

Long-term financial security

Three main types of long-term saving were identified as a priority in the previous chapter: providing financial security for children in the event of the death of a parent; saving money to give children a start in adult life; and saving for old age.

In particular, they wanted products for these purposes which:

- are simple and transparent so that the money saved can easily be calculated;

- offer automatic saving of small amounts weekly or fortnightly;

- but are flexible so that payments can be suspended during times of financial hardship, without incurring penalties;

- give only restricted access to the money saved;

- can be used as collateral for small loans if required.

Again, they recognised that their requirements could be costly and they were prepared to accept lower returns for more appropriate products.

The most common ways for low-income households to consider providing long-term financial security is through insurance policies and these were the products on which the focus group participants concentrated their discussion.

Security for families and children

Term insurance was the only way that participants considered providing for their children in the event of their death and, in many respects, these policies meet the needs they identified. They are simple and transparent and, if bought from home service agents, the premiums could be paid in small regular amounts. Even so, some participants misunderstood the terms and felt they had got poor value for money when the term of the policy ended and they were still alive!

> "You shell out and shell out and then you find once they're 16 [the company says], 'Sorry, you get nothing back at the end of it' and the insurance companies do very well, thank you very much, on your money. But that's not good enough, it's a case of, if anything happens to mum or dad you need to know that they're going to be provided for."

Likewise, many of the group participants thought first of a life insurance policy if they wanted to provide long-term savings for their children. Sold through home service companies, these offer a routine and disciplined way of saving small sums of money. They also give only restricted access to the money saved. Consequently, a number of the group participants and the people interviewed in-depth had, in the past, taken out policies in their children's names.

Concerns about such policies, however, focused around their early surrender value.

> "I had insurance policies and I got into a bit of debt, I ended up having to cash them in and that was the worst day's work I've ever done ... I only had to do three more years and then I would have had a substantial amount more, but I just needed it at the time. I got out less than what I paid in. I've got nothing for my kids now."

Experiences such as this are commonplace among low-income households, with research showing that cashing in insurance policies is one of the earliest strategies for making ends meet following a drop in income (Kempson et al, 1994). The 1998 Personal Investment Authority Consumer Panel Report draws attention to the low level of persistency of life insurance policies. This shows that four years after they had been taken out, 38% of life insurance policies sold through home service companies had been surrendered, as had 23% of policies sold by company representatives (Personal Investment Authority, 1998). Moreover, industry-based research by LIMRA shows that rates of persistency are strongly linked to incomes (LIMRA, 1996).

This raises some important issues. First, life insurance policies are not transparent, so that households do not know, at any one time, what the surrender value of their policy would be. Second, they are ill-suited to the needs of households with low and fluctuating incomes. In part, this is because of the in-built inflexibility of payments – under the Industrial Life Assurance Act policies have either to be paid up or lapsed if the policy holder has missed more than seven payments. However, it is also because the costs are front-loaded and, if they surrender their policy early, policy holders may not even get back the money they have paid in. Many of these costs relate to the compliance with regulations.

In view of these misgivings, it is appropriate to ask if low-income households should be saving in this way and whether saving in a bank or building society account would be a better option. The first response to this question is that such households are frequently *sold* insurance policies, while they seldom receive marketing or sales approaches for bank or building society savings accounts. Second, saving with a bank or building society is not a disciplined routine and, if money is short, the temptation not to save is often too great. Third, access to money can be too easy unless a limited access account is opened. Fourth, there are frequently problems of access to accounts themselves. Banks and building societies seldom have branches nearby poor neighbourhoods and, to defend their mutual status, many building societies have had to impose minimum deposits to open an account.

Given that the wish to save for children often went hand-in-hand with a desire to provide for them should their parent die, there is a need for a simple and transparent product to meet both these needs. Such products already exist, but they are often far from transparent. The key to its suitability, however, would be routine payments, limited access to savings and no penalties for early surrender. One suggestion, put forward by some of the group participants, was the possibility of using savings products as security for cash loans at times of need. This would enable them to retain savings *and* avoid the necessity of paying the high charges of door-to-door moneylenders.

> "I cashed mine [insurance policy] and my pension, both.... If I could have borrowed on it when you needed it, then that would have been fine. But I never. So, I've got to start everything from scratch."

Credit unions could, potentially, meet this need as, once they have an established pattern of saving, members can apply for a loan that is proportional to the amount they have saved. It would, however, require further development of the credit union service to provide the discipline of regular saving and limited access to funds that attract people to life insurance and also to

include insurance to cover the death of a parent. It would also depend on a considerable extension of the availability of credit unions in low-income communities. Alternatively, other mutual organisations might well be in a position to explore new products to meet this need.

Security for old age

Even though providing for their old age was one of the main priorities for older people, only a very small number of people in the focus groups or who were interviewed in-depth had either first- or second-hand experience of private pensions. Even so, there was widespread unease about private pensions, which focused on three main issues.

First, pensions were seen as complex products that group participants found hard to understand.

> "I don't think I've had enough information on it, about getting personal pensions and things like that. I've got a pension through my work, but I don't think that would be very much anyway.... I think I can probably top it up and things like that, but I've not really had any information on it off anybody about increasing your pension. I think the information people get is non-existent."

This concern was fuelled by the very real fears engendered by pensions mis-selling, such that people were worried about actually taking out a pension themselves.

Second, those who had had private pensions in the past drew attention to their lack of transparency. Personal pensions were particularly criticised in this regard and the people who had experience of them cited how it was impossible to find out how much pension one might expect to get. There was, however, similar confusion about occupational pensions.

Third, there was concern about not being able to keep up a continuous payment record. There was confusion among those not working about what had happened to past payments and a belief that these had been lost. There was also concern that people with a chequered working career may never be able to put enough by for a decent pension.

A basic, guaranteed pension, into which people pay while they are in work, but have payments maintained by the State when they are out of paid employment, would go a long way towards overcoming these concerns.

Medium-term financial security

Provision for job loss or damage or loss of household items was only a priority for a small number of the group participants and there was little experience of financial products to meet either of these needs. As a consequence there was much less discussion of how they might best be met. However, some of the depth interview scripts were drawn from a study of access to home contents insurance and these have been drawn upon to give a clearer indication of how well existing insurance products meet the needs of low-income households.

Home contents insurance

Affordability is the key issue with regard to home contents insurance, and this has two important dimensions. First, there is the high premiums that many low-income households face because they live in areas where the risk of burglaries (and insurance claims) is high. Second, there are real problems associated with paying an annual premium and the limited possibilities for spreading the costs across the year.

The first difficulty can, potentially, be overcome in two ways: through cheaper policies with less comprehensive cover and through broadening the risk pool. Some low-income households would welcome indemnity insurance (second-hand replacement instead of new-for-old), yet such policies are increasingly difficult to find. Others would be satisfied with catastrophe-only insurance to cover them for fire and flood but not burglary. The insurance industry, however, says that where they are available such policies are not widely popular.

The other solution, therefore, is to widen the pool of risk. This clearly runs against the general trend in the insurance industry which is towards risk assessment being made on smaller

geographical areas. There are, however, interesting developments with local authorities offering *insure with rent* schemes to their tenants which reverse this trend. Because they act as intermediaries, local authorities can pass the commission on to their tenants in the form of lower premiums. Indeed, experience with block policies, where all tenants are offered the same premium, shows that even the lowest risk tenants get cover at a lower price than if they insured direct with an insurance company (Whyley et al, 1998).

Intermediary schemes also offer opportunities for policy holders to spread the cost of the premiums. Local authorities, for example, collect premiums on a weekly or fortnightly basis along with the rent.

One of the focus groups was held in a local authority housing estate which had an *insure with rent* scheme. The participants were agreed that this was an excellent development, but hardly any of them had taken out a policy. This emphasises that take-up of such schemes will be far from universal because, as the previous chapter highlighted, home contents insurance is a lower priority than other savings and insurance products.

Insurance against job loss

Although it was a high priority for some of the group participants, insurance against job loss was an abstract aspiration and there was little discussion of how it might be provided.

It is clear, however, that there would be very real problems of access and affordability among households on the margins of financial services. They are not the types of people that insurance companies would be keen to recruit as customers, as they mostly have unstable work histories or have experienced long periods of unemployment. So, if they could get a policy at all, it would almost certainly be at a price they could not afford.

Research into mortgage payment protection policies also suggests that low-income households might be offered policies which would limit their likelihood of a successful claim. Exclusions for pre-existing medical conditions and insecure employment currently lead to three out of 10 claims on mortgage payment protection policies being rejected (Ford and Kempson, 1997; Kempson et al, 1999: forthcoming). People who would be subject to such exclusionary clauses are greatly over-represented among those on the margins of financial services, compared with the types of household likely to have a mortgage. Indeed, just about all the group participants who gave insurance against job loss a high priority were currently out of work.

Nevertheless, it is important to recognise that people who are virtually uninsurable in the private sector do feel that they want to make provision against future job loss if they return to employment. They have little expectation of help from the State, which they anticipate being eroded even further, from a level that they have already experienced as being inadequate. This raises some important questions for future welfare reform.

Short-term credit

The previous chapter showed that, although consumer credit was a low priority for the focus group participants, it was the subject of considerable discussion largely because it is hard for low-income households to avoid. Credit is needed largely to replace essential household goods and to smooth the peaks and troughs of a household budget.

This area of provision is subject to more access difficulties than any other type of financial product. Few households who are on the margins of financial services find it easy to get access to high street credit. Indeed, there were many examples of people, in both the focus groups and depth interviews, who had had credit applications turned down. An assessment of the appropriateness of existing sources of credit must encompass the many forms which are available. For simplicity's sake, we have grouped these into revolving credit (overdraft facilities and credit cards); one-off credit agreements tied to the purchase of goods; and cash loans.

If they can get access, mail order catalogues or the government's Social Fund provide low-income households with the most appropriate form of credit for purchasing goods. Both sources are interest-free, and offer the best value for money, although goods bought through mail order can cost more than they would in the shops. They are relatively simple and transparent products that are associated with reputable providers. They also have the most appropriate methods of payment: Social Fund repayments are deducted at source from benefit payments, while local agents collect repayments for mail order companies. The chief drawback lies in their lack of flexibility over repayments.

There are, however, more problems with regard to credit required to make ends meet. Yet the majority of low-income households express a greater need for small amounts of cash, to smooth their budget, than for credit tied to particular goods. People in the focus groups were adamant that, even if they could get access, they did not want to use overdrafts or credit cards, because of their lack of transparency and the consequent risk of losing control of their budget. In their circumstances, one-off loans with fixed payments give them greater control and have an in-built repayment schedule. Yet this form of credit can be much harder for them to gain access to, particularly at good value for money. Banks and building societies are generally perceived to be the most reputable providers of cash loans. Yet few low-income households are likely to be able to obtain loans from them and banks and building societies would not, in any case, be prepared to offer the small sums they require.

Consequently, those in need of a cash loan have no choice but to use moneylenders. Few people saw them as reputable lenders, but they were often the only provider willing and able to meet their needs. They offer simple products, with flexible terms and realistic methods of repayment. The flipside of this, however, is that credit obtained from moneylenders is generally very expensive. Interest rates range from 100-500%, with the higher rates charged for smaller and shorter-term loans (Rowlingson, 1994).

6

Summary and policy implications

Despite a steady increase both in the number of households using financial services, and in the range of products they use, around 1.5 million households in Britain (7%) lack any financial products at all and a further 4 million (19%) have only one or two. These households are drawn from many walks of life but the majority are single-person or lone-parent households; live in social rented housing; have no one in work and, consequently, live on low incomes drawn largely from state benefits.

The *likelihood* of being on the margins of financial services clearly depends on who you are, but where you live is also important. The types of household most likely to be marginalised are those headed by very young or very old people; by lone parents or (to a lesser degree) single pensioners; and by African-Caribbean, Pakistani or Bangladeshi people. Above all they are the poorest households in Britain: those where the head of household is unemployed, sick or disabled; with net incomes of between £50 and £150 a week, especially if they claim Income Support, supplemented by Housing Benefit. Levels of use of financial products are lowest among households living in council housing or housing association properties; in local authorities where there is a high level of deprivation; and especially in Scotland, the North of England or Greater London.

Statistical modelling, however, shows that non- and low-use of financial products is largely explained by four main factors: low net household income; receipt of income-related benefits; length of time since the head of household has been in paid work; and housing tenure. Beyond this, being a single non-pensioner, being Pakistani or Bangladeshi, and

having left school before the age of 16, were also highly significant in increasing the chances of being without financial products. So, too, were living in Scotland, Wales or Greater London, or in one of the 50 most deprived local authorities in England and Wales.

Levels of non-use of specific types of financial product are a great deal higher than the overall levels of non-use. Between one in eight and one in five households do not have a current account; one in five have no insurance policies; a quarter have no savings or investment products and a similar proportion have no credit commitments; and a third of households have no private pension provision. In general, use of specific financial products follows the overall pattern of use, for example, increasing with the level of income. There is, however, evidence of a hierarchy of products. People who have only one or two are most likely to have a current account or savings accounts with a building society and bank. Beyond that they either have an occupational pension or have insured the structure of their home. Insurance provision for ill-health or loss of income is very rare among those who are most excluded, as are most investment products (TESSAs, PEPs, unit trusts etc) and private medical insurance.

The processes of exclusion

There is no single explanation for households being on the margins of financial services. Moreover, it is clearly a dynamic process with many more households moving in and out of using financial products than lack access at any one time. Although three quarters of them have never used financial services to any degree, a quarter have been users in the past. And even among those who have never been users, some will almost certainly do so at some stage in their lives.

Those who have never really been engaged with financial services fall into five main groups. First, there are elderly people (aged over 70) who are part of a cash-only generation. Second, we have young householders who have not *yet* engaged with financial services, but may do so once they have a foothold in the labour market. The third group is women who became single mothers at an early age, before they had a chance to get a secure job and start using financial services. Fourth, and the largest group of all, are householders (single people and couples) who have never really had a secure job that has permitted them to begin using financial services. And, finally, there are some ethnic groups – Pakistani and Bangladeshi households in particular – where language, religion and lack of knowledge limits use. In general the factors that inhibit these people starting to use financial services include: being unable to get a secure foothold in the labour market; having parents who do not use financial services; and living in a marginalised community.

People stop using financial services either when they experience a substantial drop in income, or when women separate or are widowed, and their former partner had all financial products in his name. Following a drop in income, some people choose to close down all their financial products in order to balance their budget and keep tight control over their money. Others, however, only do so once they have fallen into financial difficulties and are often forced to do so by suppliers withdrawing the facilities. Likewise, some women left without any financial products choose not to apply for replacements in their own name as they want to retain control over their finances. But others either apply and are turned down or do not apply as they believe they would be refused. Most of these people would re-engage with financial services if they experienced an increase in income, which is usually associated with getting paid work.

On the whole, then, large numbers of households are not being denied access to all forms of financial service provision; nor have they made an unconstrained choice to opt out. Instead, most of them face a range of barriers. This includes *price exclusion* – where some

financial services are too expensive; *condition exclusion* – where the conditions attached to products make them inappropriate for their needs; and *marketing exclusion* – with no one trying to sell them financial products.

In addition, financial exclusion is encouraged in a range of ways by government policy and practice. This ranges from the key finding that being in receipt of means-tested benefits greatly increases the odds of a household being without financial products, to the ways that legislation and regulation can act to limit access to particular financial products or increase their costs.

Unmet needs and the consequences of financial exclusion

This analysis raises an important question, *Does it matter that a small minority of households do not use financial services?* Ironically, as the numbers of households affected decreases, so the depth of the problems they face seems to increase. Managing a cash budget, with no insurance, long-term investments or pension, matters more when these have become an accepted way for the great majority of households to manage their affairs. Indeed, lacking financial products can contribute to more general social exclusion and most households in this position identify key areas of unmet need.

Broadly, there were two main areas of unmet need for financial services: for day-to-day money management and for long-term financial security. Medium-term security – insurance against loss of income, or loss or damage to possessions – was of secondary importance. In contrast, there was very little expressed need for savings or consumer credit products to help with buying more expensive items. Indeed, there was considerable resistance to consumer credit per se.

Being without a current account means households deal entirely in cash. This complicates the process of bill payment, incurs charges for paying in cash, and often means that they pay far more for basic services, such as fuel. It causes problems when people need to issue a cheque and, more so, when they need to cash one. Lacking access to short-term credit to smooth the peaks and troughs of the household budget makes budgeting more difficult and can lead to arrears or the use of high-cost moneylenders.

Lack of long-term financial security is a particular concern, as people expect State provision to decline still further in the future. Parents tend to put their children's needs first; only later do they begin to think about providing for their old age. Few expect to receive much in the way of a State pension and anticipate having to continue to work or face very real poverty.

Although medium-term security was less important, a minority of younger people were concerned about providing themselves with a way of supplementing State benefits while they were unable to work. Interestingly, these were almost all people who were looking for work and wanted to avoid ever falling back into the same financial circumstances in the future. Home contents insurance is almost invariably a second priority, if it is given any priority at all. Concerns here centre on the fact that replacing stolen or damaged goods is almost impossible for those living on a low income, with no money put by in savings and only limited access to consumer credit.

There is widespread resistance to the use of consumer credit among those on the margins of financial services, coupled with an acceptance that 'lumpy' expenditure could not be met without it. Limited access to high street credit means either using though a third party or, more commonly, relying on high-cost door-to-door moneylenders.

Meeting the needs

Meeting the needs of households that currently lack financial products is not necessarily an insurmountable problem. The evidence suggests that their requirements are not greatly different from other consumers and that, although most products fail to meet the design and delivery needs of low-income households, it would not require major changes to make them more appropriate

While opinions among focus group participants differed as to which organisations would make

the most responsible providers, the key criteria were that they are secure, reputable, trustworthy and understand the needs of low-income households. Further, they expressed a strong preference for providers with a local presence in their communities. There was little support for dealing with non-mainstream financial service providers. It is likely, however, that some of their requirements could not be met by the private sector alone. In these circumstances, public–private partnerships may be the way forward. *Insure with rent* schemes, where local authorities act as intermediaries offering home contents insurance to tenants, are a good example of ways that the public sector can work with private companies to widen access to financial services.

Focus group participants identified a number of key requirements for product design which apply broadly across all financial products. Some were, in fact, little different from those of other consumers: simplicity and transparency; cost and value for money; appropriate marketing. Others, such as flexibility and appropriate delivery mechanisms, are particular to low-income households. They recognised that these elements may, in some circumstances, be incompatible and that they may have to make trade-offs between them. They also acknowledged that some of their requirements, particularly those relating to product delivery, would be costly. They expressed a willingness to meet these costs, where they were perceived to be reasonable, on the grounds that they already pay more for facilities such as pre-payment meters and doorstep credit facilities, which are specifically designed to meet their needs.

Day-to-day money management

Although current accounts could provide access to all the needs identified by focus group participants for day-to-day money management they have two key design faults. First, because the vast majority of current accounts provide access to credit, even if only in the form of unauthorised overdrafts. As a consequence they are not freely available to all and households on low and fluctuating incomes are constantly concerned about inadvertently overdrawing. Second, they lack transparency when used for money transactions. This is a particular problem where people face financial penalties for unauthorised overdrawing.

A simple savings accounts could overcome some of these difficulties but some require minimum deposits which would place them out of reach of most people with low incomes. More particularly, they do not provide a way of paying bills. Focus group participants wanted a means of spreading bills into weekly or fortnightly installments, preferably deducted from their income. These needs could be fulfilled by the type of 'budgeting account' which used to be available, but which has come to be replaced by direct debits.

Consequently, what is needed is a product which falls somewhere between a current account and a savings account; one that is simple and transparent; provides basic money transfer functions, including a way of paying bills; cannot be overdrawn but offers a 'buffer zone' permitting the account to go into the red by a small amount for a few days.

Long-term financial security

Products offering longer-term financial security were also not quite appropriate for low-income households. Term insurance and life insurance, used to provide security for families and children, could meet some of the criteria, particularly when sold through home service companies. However, some focus group participants had taken out term insurance without fully understanding its purpose and therefore felt they had got poor value-for-money. In addition, life insurance policies are not transparent and are ill-suited to the needs of households with low and fluctuating incomes. While these problems may suggest that low-income households would be better saving in a bank or building society account, they, too, do not fully meet the identified needs. Compared with life insurance, they are much less commonly marketed to households on the margins of financial services. Furthermore, they do not offer a disciplined saving routine, and access to the money saved is too easy.

A simple product offering a means of both saving for children and the option of including provision for them should their parent die could meet these needs. It should be based on

routine payments; limited access to money; and avoid the penalties of early surrender. Allowing savings products to be used as security for cash loans would permit low-income households to retain long-term savings without needing to borrow from moneylenders at high interest rates. Credit unions could potentially meet this need, although it would require a further development of their service and a considerable extension of their availability. Alternatively, new products could be developed by other mutual organisations.

Pensions were perceived to be more problematic by focus group participants. In particular, they were viewed as too complex to understand and lacking in transparency. Many people were also concerned that they would be unable to maintain a continuous payment record. The basic stakeholder pension, currently being proposed by the Department of Social Security, could overcome many of these concerns, at least for those on modest incomes. Its availability would, however, need to be extended to people with incomes under £9,000 a year, if it is to meet the needs of people currently on the margins of financial services.

Medium-term financial security

Products offering medium-term security, such as home contents insurance and insurance against job loss, have problems of both access and affordability. Cheaper policies, with less comprehensive cover, or moves to widen the risk pool, would increase take-up of home contents insurance policies. Interesting developments among local authorities offering *insure with rent* schemes suggest that intermediary schemes can successfully deliver this type of insurance to low-income households. It will, however, always be one of the lower priorities for expenditure by low-income households.

It is more difficult to see how insurance against job loss could be extended to all households, although it was a high priority for some people in the focus groups. If people with long-term health problems and unstable work histories cannot be provided for by the private sector, this raises some important questions for future welfare reform.

Short-term credit

Finally, despite the relatively diverse range of credit provision, low-income households are extremely likely to be channelled towards the types which they least want to use. Very few low-income households can gain access to mainstream credit provision, and experience of direct refusal is higher in relation to credit than to any other product. Easiest to access to is credit linked to the purchase of goods, such as hire purchase, catalogues and the Social Fund. Yet people on low incomes express the greatest need for relatively small amounts of credit, in cash, to smooth the household budget. For this, they can only really turn to moneylenders who are willing to provide them with credit with flexible terms and realistic payment methods. Yet this form of credit is seen as offering very poor value for money, with interest rates ranging from 100-500%, with the higher rates charged for smaller and shorter-term loans.

The policy implications

The key questions raised by this research are: *how many people might be brought into financial services?* and, *how can it be encouraged?* To answer these, it is helpful to return to the main categories of people who are currently on the margins of financial services.

The most difficult group is the elderly cash-only generation, who account for 230,000 of households with no financial products and a further 615,000 of those making little use of financial services. It seems unlikely that, having reached their 70s or 80s, they will begin to use financial products for the first time. Indeed, it is among this group that there is greatest resistance to managing their financial affairs in any other way.

At the other extreme, those who are, potentially, the easiest to bring into using financial services are young householders who have not *yet* started to use financial products (especially if their parents are users) and those who have had them in the past but given them up to keep control following a change in circumstances.

Young people represent 125,000 of households with no financial products and 335,000 of households making minimal use of financial services. They need ways to engage them earlier in their adult lives. This means low-cost, simple, 'no frills' financial products, with a minimum of risk assessment, that can be stepped up as their financial position improves. But they also need better information and education, particularly if their parents made little or no use of financial services.

In contrast, households that have stopped using financial services in response to a drop in income require more flexible and transparent products, with more realistic payment methods which offer, in particular, ways of spreading costs more evenly. They account for 190,000 of the non-users and 505,000 low users.

Other groups provide the biggest challenge to increasing access to financial services, as traditionally they have been the people who are least attractive to financial service providers. They include people on the margins of the labour market, who have either been out of work long term or in and out of insecure, low-paid jobs (585,000 non-users and 1.56 million low users); women who were single mothers at an early age (150,000 non-users; 400,000 low users); and people who have been denied financial products following a change in circumstance (190,000 non-users and 505,000 low users).

These three groups have broadly similar needs. Like the young householders, they need simple, low-cost products that involve the minimum of risk assessment. But, like the householders who have disengaged following a change in circumstance, they need products that are flexible, transparent and offer payment methods that fit their existing systems of money management. They will also need much more encouragement to start using financial services than either of these other two groups.

Finally, there is a group of Pakistani and Bangladeshi households (around 60,000 non-users and 160,000 of those with only one or two products) who will share many of these needs but also require financial products that meet the teaching of Islam. Moreover, financial service providers have to tackle the language and cultural problems such households face accessing their products.

Bringing this together, there are four key issues with regard to achieving greater use of financial services: reducing barriers to access; product design; delivery of services; and encouraging take-up, including the need for information and advice. While much of the responsibility for tackling these issues will lie with private sector providers, others also have an important part to play. This includes government and regulators as well as individual consumers themselves.

Reducing barriers to access

To widen access it is necessary to overcome the barriers associated with risk assessment and improving physical access. It is clearly unrealistic to expect a reversal of the trend towards more precise risk assessment; instead we need to look at product design and delivery to achieve the same effect. Examples would include the design of current accounts which offer a range of money transaction services but no direct access to credit. These could then be offered with minimal credit scoring or none at all. As regards credit facilities, it might include lending small sums, but increasing the amount in line with payment records. Use of intermediaries, such as local authorities, to deliver insurance products widens the risk pool and widens access.

Similarly, using intermediaries to deliver financial products can overcome the problems of physical access. Telephone and computer-based services, however, are likely to reinforce financial exclusion as a very large proportion of excluded households lack these facilities.

Product design

On the whole, people who are currently on the margins of financial services do not have unrealistic needs. And, although at present few financial products meet these needs, in most cases it would not take much redesign to make them more appropriate.

In terms of day-to-day money management this means an account that is simple but allows users to retain tight control over their money. It would offer basic money transfer facilities, including a facility for spreading the cost of bills. It should carry no credit facilities but have a buffer zone to allow some flexibility. Ideally, it should also be designed so that it can be

made available without the need for credit scoring.

Products offering longer-term financial security need to be simple and transparent so that users can assess exactly how much they have saved and incur lower costs associated with regulation compliance. They should be based on regular and automatic saving; flexible so that products can be retained even during times of hardship; and give restricted access to the money saved. To increase persistency rates long-term savings products could be used as collateral for small loans.

For home contents insurance the key issue is one of affordability. In terms of product design it means wider availability of simpler, cheaper products such as indemnity insurance (second-hand replacement value rather than new-for-old), or unbundled policies for catastrophe only.

The type of short-term credit facilities needed are ones that offer small, one-off, fixed-term loans rather than revolving credit, fixed and automatic payments, and take advantage of developments in technology to allow much lower APRs than are currently available from moneylenders.

Finally, there is an unmet need for financial products that meet the requirements of Islam.

Delivery systems

People who are on the margins of financial services want to deal with organisations that are financially secure, trustworthy and understand their needs. It is not, however, necessary for the same organisation to both provide the product and deliver it to the customer. But with the decline in bank branches, reduction in home collection services for insurance and resentment at the costs of weekly collected credit, we need to find other ways of delivering financial products to the people who need them.

The real issue here is how to replicate the virtues of the traditional ways of delivering financial products through home service agents while keeping down the costs. Experience shows that the use of intermediaries offers many advantages. For example, many local authorities run *insure with rent* schemes for tenants wanting home contents policies, which they are able to offer at a substantial saving on similar policies bought direct or through a broker. The Post Office is also exploring a similar role as financial service intermediary, as are a small number of credit unions and housing associations.

Potential users of such services recognise that they may need to pay extra for more tailor-made forms of delivery. But the experiences of PayPoint show that there may be other beneficiaries of such new developments who could be expected to meet some of the costs. PayPoint is able to offer a free service to customers wanting to pay household bills in cash as the creditors meet all the costs.

The costs of delivery can also be contained through economies of scale if a supplier offers more than one product to a household, allowing them to create bundles of products to suit their needs. This may be one way of retaining existing home service providers and reducing their charges.

New technology offers some opportunities for the delivery of products at this end of the market. Electronic cards and electronic money transmissions are likely to be the most acceptable. In contrast, the low levels of telephone and computer ownership among households on the margins of financial services would rule out solutions such as call centres, telebanking and on-line banking.

Encouraging take-up

Levels of knowledge of the types of product available is remarkably low among households that make little use of financial services. This is reinforced by very low levels of marketing of the sort of products such households need, which leads them to believe that financial services are not for the poor.

Encouraging take-up therefore has to start by tackling the widespread mistrust of many financial providers, which is greatest towards those that are geographically remote. Use of trusted intermediaries could well go some way towards overcoming these barriers. However, there is also a need to address the fact that the current payment of State benefits seems to encourage disengagement from financial services. This is not a simple matter to tackle,

as, among other things, it has implications for the viability of many small community and sub-Post Offices. But it is not an insurmountable problem if the Post Office were to take on a more active role as financial service intermediary.

Targeted marketing and delivery of new products as they become available would, of course, increase their take-up. But it does need to take into account the language and cultural barriers faced by some potential users, and those from the Pakistani and Bangladeshi communities in particular. Literature in the languages of main minority groups and more ethnic minority staff engaged in the delivery of products would both be desirable.

The growing complexity of financial service provision means that consumers, generally, say they need a source of independent information and advice before making purchases of financial products (see for example, Personal Investment Authority, 1998; Rowlingson et al, 1999: forthcoming). This need is especially acute among those who currently make little or no use of financial services, many of whom have very low levels of knowledge and almost no experience to draw on when deciding which products to acquire. This makes them especially vulnerable to mis-selling and encourages self-exclusion. The Tax Aid service could well act a model for developing such independent financial advice.

Legislation and government policy

As already noted, financial exclusion is inadvertently encouraged by government policy and practice in a range of ways. Payment of means-tested social security benefits by giro or order book clearly encourages out-of-work recipients to operate a cash budget. In contrast, the move away from cash wages has acted to increase the use of bank and building society accounts by those in work. Moves towards automatic cash transfer (ACT) of benefits will, however, need to be made cautiously, not least because of the potential impact on the network of sub- and community Post Offices that rely on income from processing benefit payments.

Second, there is a need for a specific review of the regulation of financial services to identify where it may cause or reinforce financial exclusion. A number of specific examples were drawn to our attention in the course of this research; there will almost certainly be others.

For example, the costs of compliance with regulation means that many savings products are made less affordable to low-income households with only small sums of money to invest. If simpler products are designed there is a parallel need to review the level of regulation they require. This issue was raised by the then Deregulation Task Force in its 1996 report.

Other legislation places restrictions on product design and delivery that increases their inaccessibility or inappropriateness to low-income households. The need to comply with money laundering regulations, for example, means that some people are denied access to bank or building society accounts because they lack a permanent address. On the other hand, the lack of regulation to prevent carpet-bagging means that building societies have to address the issue by requiring minimum initial deposits, so excluding low-income households with only modest amounts to open an account. While under the Industrial Insurance Act, if a policy holder misses seven payments a policy must either be paid up or lapsed. Consequently, life insurance policies cannot offer the degree of flexibility required by households on low and fluctuating incomes. This same Act precludes payment of premiums by direct debt.

Finally, government policies can create a new market for financial services. The proposed stakeholder pension is a good example. At the same time, future welfare reform needs to address the extent to which it may be adding to the problem of financial exclusion, rather than addressing it. Experience with cut backs to Income Support for Mortgage Interest, with the intention of increasing take-up of private mortgage payment protection insurance, has been far from encouraging. It is the most vulnerable homeowners, who are least attractive to insurance companies and have fewest resources to call upon while out of work, who have been adversely affected by the changes (Kempson et al, 1999).

Moving forward

Since this research was started there have been a number of significant developments that signify a willingness by a wide range of organisations to tackle the problem of 'financial exclusion'. Indeed, the climate of opinion is more disposed to tackling the problem than at any time in the past.

There have been a number of private sector initiatives. The British Bankers Association, Association of British Insurers and Building Societies Association all have committees reviewing how far their members are able to address the problem of financial exclusion. The British Bankers Association has recently commissioned a study of access to current accounts. A number of banks and building societies are developing new products designed to meet the needs we have outlined in this report. The Association of British Insurers has, similarly, commissioned research and has organised a conference on social and financial exclusion.

Similarly there are many public sector initiatives, and tackling financial exclusion is firmly on the government's agenda. Arising from the work of the Social Exclusion Unit, there is a Policy Action Team on access to financial services and a Task Force on support for credit unions from banks and building societies. Both are looking at practical solutions to financial exclusion. The Office of Fair Trading has published a report on *Vulnerable consumers and financial services* (1999). The Treasury has issued a consultation document *Proposed amendments to the Credit Unions Act 1979*, seeking views on ways of increasing the number of credit unions, on ways of allowing them to offer a wider range of services and on future regulation of the credit union movement. And the Financial Services Authority has also published a consultation document – on *Promoting public understanding of financial services*.

In addition, there have been a number of initiatives that would stimulate new markets. Individual Savings Accounts (ISAs) are one such example, as is the stakeholder pension, although, as they are currently designed, neither may actually meet the needs of those on the margins of financial services. Local authorities, too, have helped create new markets, for example, through the setting up of *insure with rent* schemes. The proposed changes to the status of the Post Office will enable it to develop its role as a financial services intermediary and this, too, may help to stimulate new demands for financial services.

The creation of the Financial Services Authority brings together regulation of financial services and will extend the Personal Investment Authority objectives of ensuring that regulation protects the most vulnerable at a cost they can afford. It also has a wide ranging brief to deal with consumer information, advice and education.

Overall, current thinking is based on three main premises that this research would endorse. First, that people who are currently on the margins of financial services should be integrated into mainstream provision, wherever possible. Following from this is a commitment to the private sector being encouraged to develop new products and services to meet unmet needs. The possibility of using legislation to combat financial exclusion is being retained by government as a last resort. Finally, there is widespread commitment to increasing access to financial services through a public/ private partnership: with the private sector developing new products; central government creating new markets, addressing issues related to regulation, and providing subsidy where this is needed; and local government and other not-for profit bodies helping to deliver financial services to those who are currently excluded.

References

Berthoud, R. and Kempson, E. (1992) *Credit and debt: The PSI Report*, London: Policy Studies Institute.

Burchardt, T. and Hills, J. (1997) *Private welfare insurance and social security: Pushing the boundaries*, York: York Publishing Services.

Ford, J. and Kempson, E. (1997) *Bridging the gap: Safety nets for home buyers*, York: Centre for Housing Policy, University of York.

Ford, J. and Rowlingson, K. (1996) 'Low income households and credit: exclusion, preference and inclusion', *Environment and Planning A*, vol 28, pp 1345-60.

Herbert, A. and Kempson, E. (1996) *Credit use and ethnic minorities*, London: Policy Studies Institute.

Kempson, E. (1994) *Outside the banking system: A review of households without a current account*, London: HMSO.

Kempson, E. (1996) *Life on a low income*, York: York Publishing Services.

Kempson, E. (1998) *Savings and low income and ethnic minority households*, London: Personal Investment Authority.

Kempson, E. and Whyley, C. (1998) *Access to current accounts*, London: British Bankers Association.

Kempson, E. and Whyley, C. (1999a) *The extent and nature of financial exclusion*, Working Paper 1, Bristol: Personal Finance Research Centre, University of Bristol.

Kempson, E. and Whyley, C. (1999b) *The processes and consequences of financial exclusion*, Working Paper 2, Bristol: Personal Finance Research Centre, University of Bristol.

Kempson, E., Bryson, A. and Rowlingson, K. (1994) *Hard times? How poor families make ends meet*, London: Policy Studies Institute.

Kempson, E., Ford, J. and Quilgers, D. (1999: forthcoming) *Unsafe safety nets. The effectiveness of safety nets for mortgagors*, York: Centre for Housing Policy, University of York.

Leyshon, A. and Thrift, N. (1993) 'The restructuring of the UK financial services industry in the 1990s: a reversal of fortune?', *Journal of Rural Studies*, vol 9, no 3, pp 223-41.

Leyshon, A. and Thrift, N. (1994) 'Access to financial services and financial infrastructure withdrawal: problems and policies', *Area*, vol 16, no 3, pp 268-75.

Leyshon, A. and Thrift, N. (1995) 'Geographies of financial exclusion: financial abandonment in Britain and the United States', *Transactions of the Institute of British Geographers*, New Series, vol 20, pp 312-41.

LIMRA (1996) *Lapsation and the policy holder*, London: LIMRA.

Office of Fair Trading (1999) *Vulnerable consumers and financial services: The report of the Director General's Inquiry*, Office of Fair Trading.

Personal Investment Authority (1996) *Consumer panel report*, London: Personal Investment Authority.

Personal Investment Authority (1998) *Consumer panel report*, London: Personal Investment Authority.

Rowlingson, K. (1994) *Moneylenders and their customers*, London: Policy Studies Institute.

Rowlingson, K., Whyley, C. and Warren, T. (1999: forthcoming) *Securing a future: The links between income and assets*, London: Policy Studies Institute.

Whyley, C. and Kempson, E. (1998) *Frequent payers and pre-payment meter customers in a competitive gas market*, London: Gas Consumers Council.

Whyley, C. and Kempson, E. (1999) *Meeting the needs of financially excluded households*, Working Paper 3, Bristol: Personal Finance Research Centre, University of Bristol.

Whyley, C., McCormick, J. and Kempson, E. (1998) *Paying for peace of mind: Access to home contents insurance for low-income households*, London: Policy Studies Institute.

Appendix A: Regression models

In all, six separate regression models were run: three showing the multiplicative odds of being without any products (Table 1); and three similar models showing the multiplicative odds of having two or fewer financial products (Table 2).

Reference categories

The reference categories for each of the models are given below.

Models 1A and 2A: Aged 40-49; non-pensioner couple, no children; white; male; finished full-time education at 20 or older; claims no income-related benefits; net weekly income over £300 a week; currently in work; lives in South East, South West or East Anglia.

Models 1B and 2B: Aged 40-49; non-pensioner couple, no children; white; male; finished full-time education at 20 or older; claims no income-related benefits; net weekly income over £300 a week; currently in work; lives in South East, South West or East Anglia; outright owner.

Models 1C and 2C: Aged 40-49; non-pensioner couple, no children; white; male; finished full-time education at 20 or older; claims no income-related benefits; net weekly income over £300 a week; currently in work; lives in South East, South West or East Anglia; lives in the 65 least deprived local authorities.

Interpreting the models

The numbers shown in the last three columns of each table indicate the extent to which, all other things being equal, each of the factors in the left hand column affect the 'odds' of a household having no financial products at all. Where this number is greater than one, the odds of financial exclusion are increased; when it is less than one, the odds are decreased. The odds are always measured in relation to a reference category, which in this case, comprise the people who, according to cross-tabular analysis, have characteristics which make them *least* likely to be without financial products (see below).

For example, if we look at the column showing the results of Model 1A, we see the number 32.40 shown for households receiving either IS and HB, or IS, HB and CTB. This means that, even if two households have exactly the same composition, income, employment, housing and area characteristics, the fact that one of them is claiming these benefits renders that household 32 times more likely to be without any financial products than a household which is not claiming these benefits. Similarly, in Model 1A, households headed by someone aged 70-79 or 80+ have less than half the likelihood of being without financial products than households with exactly the same other characteristics but headed by somebody younger.

The statistical significance of these factors are marked with asterisks (*). One asterisk indicates that a particular characteristic is statistically significant only at the lowest level; three asterisks (***) indicate the highest level of statistical significance. Those without asterisks still have an effect in the model, but this effect is not statistically significant and therefore does not improve our understanding.

Table 1: Models showing the likelihood (multiplicative odds) of being without any financial products

	Model 1A general estimate	Model 1B excluding mortgagors	Model 1C England only
Constant	−3.58	−3.22	−3.92
Age of head of household			
16-19	1.68	1.56	1.91
20-29	1.38*	1.32*	1.45*
30-39	1.30*	1.28	1.36*
50-59	0.99	0.98	1.12
60-69	0.75	0.70	0.82
70-79	0.44***	0.42***	0.50**
80+	0.43***	0.41***	0.57*
Household composition			
Lone parent	1.44*	1.41*	1.71**
Single non-pensioner	1.81***	1.78***	2.00***
Single pensioner	1.55*	1.54*	1.79**
Pensioner couple	1.02	1.05	1.16
Couple with children	1.47*	1.42*	1.72**
Other	1.18	1.04	1.38
Ethnicity			
Black	1.30	1.29	1.21
Indian	0.92	1.11	0.87
Pakistani/Bangladeshi	2.50**	3.04***	2.31**
Other	1.23	1.03	1.17
Gender of head of household			
Female	1.01	1.02	0.95
Age finished full-time education			
17-19	1.78*	1.76*	1.85*
16 or under	3.82***	3.56***	3.66***
Benefit status			
CTB or IS or IS and CTB	2.55***	3.72***	2.90***
HB or HB and CTB	15.75***	4.75***	16.73***
IS and HB or IS and HB and CTB	32.40***	9.57***	36.07***
Net weekly income			
£201-£300	4.09***	3.16***	5.22***
£151-£200	5.64***	4.14***	7.36***
under £150	8.09***	5.85***	10.11***
Number of years since last worked			
Up to 1 year	0.90	0.98	0.81
1-2 years	1.19	1.31	1.17
2-4 years	1.86***	2.03***	1.85**
5-9 years	2.58***	2.72***	2.59***
10+ years	4.05***	4.21***	4.03***
Never worked	4.58***	4.72***	4.77***
Region			
North and North West	1.80	1.78***	1.46**
Yorkshire and Humberside	1.38*	1.34*	1.12
East and West Midlands	1.25*	1.23	1.06
Greater London	1.75***	1.61***	1.33*
Wales	1.96***	1.99***	–
Scotland	2.94***	2.70***	–
Tenure			
Local authority tenant	na	7.05***	na
Housing association tenant		5.78***	
Private tenant		5.66***	
Deprivation score			
1 (most deprived)	na	na	1.93***
2			1.54*
3			1.39
4			1.60*
5			1.43
6 (second least deprived)			1.22
Chi Square measure of fit	5,225.07	3,660.90	4,059.54
Significance	0.0000	0.0000	0.0000
Number of cases	26,435	14,886	21,481

* significance level <0.05; ** significance level <0.01; *** significance level <0.001

Table 2: Models showing the likelihood (multiplicative odds) of having no or just one or two financial products

	Model 2A general estimate	Model 2B excluding mortgagors	Model 2C England only
Constant	0.23	0.88	−0.90
Age of head of household			
16–19	15.69***	8.12**	19.3***
20–29	2.17***	1.73***	2.24***
30–39	1.32***	1.38**	1.38***
50–59	0.91	0.78*	0.97
60–69	0.81	0.56***	0.84
70–79	0.66*	0.45***	0.68*
80+	1.02	0.68*	1.05
Household composition			
Lone parent	1.37*	1.17	1.46**
Single non-pensioner	1.40*	1.19	1.44***
Single pensioner	1.27	1.08	1.41*
Pensioner couple	0.79	0.73*	0.82
Couple with children	0.92	0.83*	0.96
Other	0.97	0.64***	1.00
Ethnicity			
Black	1.80***	1.25	1.48*
Indian	1.40	2.35**	1.14
Pakistani/Bangladeshi	5.16***	16.67***	4.90***
Other	2.11***	2.34**	1.90**
Gender of head of household			
Female	1.02	1.09	1.01
Age finished full-time education			
17–19	1.12	1.25	1.16
16 or under	2.75***	2.72***	2.64***
Benefit status			
CTB, or IS, or IS and CTB	2.23***	3.34***	2.21***
HB, or HB and CTB	17.12***	3.79***	16.14***
IS and HB, or IS and HB and CTB	43.69***	8.96***	40.92***
Net weekly income			
£201–£300	2.69***	1.87***	2.72***
£151–£200	4.44***	2.75***	4.53***
under £150	6.56***	4.27***	6.58***
Number of years since last in work			
Up to 1 year	0.58***	0.67**	0.59***
1–2 years	0.63***	0.76	0.68**
2–4 years	1.14	1.26*	1.21
5–9 years	1.31**	1.52***	1.33**
10+ years	1.89***	2.09***	1.99***
Never worked	3.95***	4.12***	4.50***
Region			
North and North West	1.52***	1.62***	1.78*
Yorkshire and Humberside	1.36***	1.35**	1.06
East and West Midlands	1.24**	1.26**	1.08
Greater London	1.84***	1.40***	1.39***
Wales	1.83***	2.15***	na
Scotland	2.66***	2.17***	na
Tenure			
Local authority tenant	na	7.85***	na
Housing association tenant		5.85***	
Private tenant		5.01***	
Deprivation score			
1 (most deprived)	na	na	1.74***
2			1.39***
3			1.25*
4			1.03
5			0.89
6 (second least deprived)			0.95
Chi Square measure of fit	14,073.31	9,239.89	11,787.62
Significance	0.000	0.000	0.000
Number of cases	26,435	14,886	21,481

* significance level <0.05; ** significance level <0.01; *** significance level <0.001.

Appendix B: Research methods

Secondary analysis of the *Family Resources Survey*

The quantitative element for this research involved extensive secondary analysis of the *Family Resources Survey* (FRS) 1995/96. The FRS is a major new national household survey, sponsored by the Department of Social Security. The survey collects information from a representative sample of 26,435 private households in Britain. Within these households, 47,000 adults and 16,000 children are interviewed. The fieldwork for the survey is conducted by the Office for National Statistics (ONS) and Social and Community Planning Research (SCPR) and uses Computer Assisted Personal Interviewing (CAPI). The overall response rate for the 1995/96 FRS was 70%.

The survey collects information on income from employment, benefits, pensions as well as on different types of assets. It provides data on 23 different financial products which have been used for the analysis in this research, including:

- current accounts with a bank or building society
- other bank accounts
- other building society accounts
- Post Office accounts
- any other accounts
- National Savings certificates or bonds
- premium bonds
- Save As You Earn (SAYE) schemes
- personal pensions
- occupational pensions
- mortgages
- mortgage payment protection insurance
- personal accident insurance
- insurance for hospitalisation
- redundancy insurance
- insurance of loss of earnings through ill-health
- private medical insurance
- TESSAs
- PEPs
- unit trusts/investment trusts
- stocks and shares, bonds, debentures or other securities
- government gilt-edged stock
- structural insurance.

Secondary analysis of qualitative interviews

This analysis is based upon 87 depth interview scripts with people on the margins of financial services, identified from five previous studies, which looked at:

- how poor families make ends meet (32 scripts);
- the customers of moneylenders (7 scripts);
- credit use and ethnic minorities (18 scripts);
- households without home contents insurance (13 scripts);
- approaches to money management and bill payment (17 scripts).

None of these surveys was designed to provide a nationally representative sample, but to illustrate the range of circumstances being studied. The same, therefore, applies to the present analysis, which covered a range of different types of household, including:

- 40 lone parents;

- 23 couples with dependent children;

- 6 single people under retirement age;

- 6 couples under retirement age and without children;

- 6 pensioner couples;

- 6 single pensioners.

The preponderance of lone parents and couples with dependent children largely reflects the use of one study which concentrated on these types of household. We included them all because of the richness of the data these scripts contained. Their inclusion does not, however, introduce any bias into the analysis.

There may, however, be a geographical bias in that only two studies (moneylenders' customers and approaches to money management) covered people living in a rural area, and none of the studies included people living in Scotland, where the proportion of households with no financial products is twice the national average. These deficiencies are addressed in the focus groups.

The analysis includes interviews with 42 households that had disengaged from financial services; 45 who had either never used any mainstream financial products at all or had had only one – which was usually a savings account. Again, this should not be taken to indicate the proportions in the population as a whole. We plan to undertake secondary analysis of an ONS Omnibus which set out to measure the proportions. This analysis will be included in the final report of the study.

Focus groups

The focus groups were conducted during July 1998 in five areas of England, Scotland and Wales. The fieldwork sites were selected to include urban, suburban and rural areas.

The sample

The sample was designed to include households without any financial products at all or with just one or two products from the following list:

- current accounts with a bank or building society;

- savings accounts with a bank or building society;

- home contents insurance;

- buildings insurance;

- occupational or personal pension;

- life insurance;

- insurance for sickness or redundancy.

The sample also included quotas to ensure that each focus group consisted of a mix of householders who:

- currently had one or two of the products on the list;

- had had one of the products on the list in the past, but had stopped using them;

- had never had any of the products on the list.

Quotas were also used to ensure that the groups include both men and women, and a wide age range. People were recruited door-to-door or in the street by Plus Four Research Ltd, according to a questionnaire designed by PFRC.

The composition of the sample

In total, 32 people participated in the focus groups, and, in many respects, their characteristics and circumstances were illustrative of those found to be significant in the quantitative stage of the research (Table 1).

Table 1: Characteristics and circumstances of the sample

Characteristics of participants and their households

Sex	
Female	24
Male	8
Age*	
up to 35	17
36-45	6
46-65	7
66-74	1
75 or more	1
Family circumstances	
Lone parent	11
Single, non-pensioner	10
Couple with children	7
Couple without children	1
Single pensioner	2
Pensioner couple	1
Employment*	
Full-time employment	3
Part-time employment	7
Unemployed	4
Unable to work	7
Caring for family	7
Retired	3
Student	1

* No information for one respondent.

Table 2: Type and number of financial products in households

Financial products in household	Numbers
Current and past use of products	
Have financial products now	22
None now, but had in the past	4
Never had financial products	6
Number of financial products in the household	
2	10
1	12
0	10
Types of financial products in the household	
Current account	17
Savings account	8
Post Office account	5
Pension	4
Life insurance	3
Home contents insurance	2
Mortgage	1
Health insurance	1

Twenty-two of the participants lived in households with access to just one or two financial products, usually a current or savings accounts (Table 2). Ten people had no financial products in their household at all. In addition, around three quarters of people in the focus groups had given up one or more financial products in the past, although only four of them had been left without any products at all. Products which had been given up tended to be current or savings accounts, pensions or insurance policies. Ceasing to use a product was almost always associated with either financial difficulty – usually brought on by job loss or relationship breakdown – or a change in circumstances, such as changing jobs, getting married or starting to cohabit with a partner. People who had stopped using products, however, were mostly those who still had access to at least one financial product at the time of the research. More than half of people who had no financial products at all at the time of the research had never used any.

The group discussions

Between four and eight people took part in each focus group and the discussions lasted for approximately 90 minutes. The focus groups were moderated by PFRC and were structured around a topic guide designed by the research team. The discussions covered a range of topics including:

- needs and priorities for financial products;

- designing new financial products;

- preferences for providers of new products;

- preferences for the delivery of new products.

Throughout the discussions, participants were encouraged not to think about financial products which are actually available, but in terms of the functions they would like products to serve and how they would like them to work.

In addition, participants were asked to complete a short questionnaire to provide factual information on their personal characteristics and circumstances, employment status, financial products currently used in their household and products which have been used in the past.

Analysis

The focus groups were tape-recorded and full transcripts obtained. The data was analysed using thematic grids developed specifically to facilitate systematic analysis of qualitative data.